EXCHANGE A MILD AND MUNDANE FAITH
FOR LIFE WITH AN UNCONTAINABLE GOD

ENTER WILD

CARLOS WHITTAKER

BESTSELLING AUTHOR OF *KILL THE SPIDER*

WATERBROOK

D0029466

ENTER WILD

Details in some anecdotes and stories have been changed to protect the identities of the persons involved.

Trade Paperback ISBN 978-0-525-65400-1
eBook ISBN 978-0-525-65401-8

Published in the United States by WaterBrook, an imprint of Random House, a division of Penguin Random House LLC.

WATERBROOK® and its deer colophon are registered trademarks of Penguin Random House LLC.

Library of Congress Cataloging-in-Publication Data
Names: Whittaker, Carlos, 1973– author.
Title: Enter wild : exchange a mild and mundane faith for life with an uncontainable God / Carlos Enrique Whittaker.
Description: First edition. | Colorado Springs : WaterBrook, 2020. | Includes bibliographical references.
Identifiers: LCCN 2019035380 | ISBN 9780525654001 (trade paperback) | ISBN 9780525654018 (ebook)
Subjects: LCSH: Christian life.
Classification: LCC BV4501.3 .W479 2020 | DDC 248.4—dc23
LC record available at https://lccn.loc.gov/2019035380

Printed in the United States of America
2020—First Edition

10 9 8 7 6 5 4 3 2

SPECIAL SALES
Most WaterBrook books are available at special quantity discounts when purchased in bulk by corporations, organizations, and special-interest groups. Custom imprinting or excerpting can also be done to fit special needs. For information, please email specialmarketscms@penguin randomhouse.com.

Praise for
Enter Wild

"This book will have you thinking, laughing, praying, and shouting "Yes!" Carlos gives us the key to finding a new level of freedom and the life of faith we've wanted to believe was possible. Inspiring and energizing."

—MARK BATTERSON, *New York Times* bestselling author of *The Circle Maker* and lead pastor of National Community Church

"As Christians, we like to talk about the abundant life Jesus offers to all who believe, but do we really know what it means to live that way? In *Enter Wild,* Carlos Whittaker takes us down the path of the abundant life Jesus spoke of in John 10:10 and helps us move from safe and boring to bold and trusting in our relationship with God. Using stories from his journey, Carlos teaches with such passion and possibility to change our thought patterns and daily prayers so we can truly live an abundant life."

—LYSA TERKEURST, #1 *New York Times* bestselling author and president of Proverbs 31 Ministries

"Carlos Whittaker does love like few people I know. His passion and energy inspire me. *Enter Wild* is an invitation to the next step on our spiritual journey. I want to take that journey with him—and you should too."

—BOB GOFF, author of the *New York Times* bestsellers *Love Does* and *Everybody, Always*

"It's possible to have a saved soul yet a wasted life. But that isn't God's desire for you. In *Enter Wild,* Carlos dares you to step into a life gripped by a God who calls you into *more:* more faith, more freedom, and more victory. This book will give you the guts you need to take the next step."

—LEVI LUSKO, lead pastor of Fresh Life Church and bestselling author

"We all experience moments when abundant life seems far off and our faith feels weak. But in those times, Carlos Whittaker reminds us that God offers life to the full. Carlos speaks to what freedom and a plentiful life can look like when we step into our calling of wild faith."

—SADIE ROBERTSON HUFF, *New York Times* bestselling author, speaker, and founder of Live Original

"Carlos and I have been close in each other's lives for more than fifteen years. Watching God do what Carlos shares in this amazing book has been a thrill. It's time for you to pull up a chair at the table now and let my buddy Carlos tell you how to Enter Rest, Enter War, and Enter Wild."

—TYLER REAGIN, founder of The Life Giving Company and author of *The Life-Giving Leader*

"This book should come with a backpack because, when you open it, you're starting a new adventure! I love that 'Los calls us out of our comfort zones to explore faith in ways that are far beyond average. Buckle up with this one. You're about to be stretched, challenged, and encouraged!"

—JON ACUFF, *New York Times* bestselling author of *Finish: Give Yourself the Gift of Done*

"Brace yourself: *Enter Wild* pulls no punches. Carlos shares his deliberate journey toward freedom with wit, courage, and candor. I was drawn in from the first page and reminded that experiencing the fullness of God requires a fierce faith; not faith you have to fight for, but faith you're finally ready to receive. You'll be forever changed by this book."

—REBEKAH LYONS, bestselling author of *Rhythms of Renewal* and *You Are Free*

To Sohaila.
Your wild faith and utter dependence on
Holy Spirit is the stuff movies are made of.
Your healing is coming. And I've got my
popcorn ready to watch it unfold.
Love, Dad

Contents

PART III: ENTER WILD

Introduction

Back in 1983 there was no such thing as *VeggieTales*. The children's department at the local church didn't have moving lights or a fog-machine haze or Xboxes lined up like airline kiosks at the airport. No.

My generation grew up with much more simplistic entertainment at church. I couldn't wait for Sunday school each and every week. Mrs. Sullivan would place all of us eight-year-olds in a semicircle. Everyone would sit cross-legged except me. I'm not sure what happened to my ligaments when the good Lord made me, but I'm certain He forgot to stretch them out appropriately. Even as a young lad, I could not for the life of me sit cross-legged. I always had to sit in a chair while the rest of my classmates sat on the ground. So with this scene in mind—eight eight-year-olds sitting cross-legged in a semicircle and one eight-year-old sitting in a chair—follow me into our Sunday school lesson.

As soon as we all sat down, Mrs. Sullivan would reach behind her chair and grab the flannel board and a small zebra-printed bag. I LOVED THIS PART! Now, if you grew up in the eighties, this was *your* Sunday school entertainment jam. It was nothing more than a three-by-three-foot piece of cardboard or poster board covered in soft material. Flannel to be exact. And what was in that zebra-printed bag? It contained paper cutout characters that would magically stick to the flannel board as Mrs. Sullivan told the story.

Before she unzipped the bag, she spoke. "Okay, boys and girls. Today we are going to talk once again about Jesus and His disciples. Remember last week we learned about how they fed the five thousand?"

And I thought, *Of course, I remember that. It's all I've been thinking about all week!*

It was true. Ever since Mrs. Sullivan told us that story, I couldn't stop thinking about it. I mean, how crazy would that have been! I actually went home after hearing the story, grabbed a few fish sticks out of the freezer, and secretly prayed that God would turn two fish sticks into four. I sat them on my Transformers plate and clenched my eyes shut.

"Dear Jesus, DO IT!" I prayed aloud. When I opened my eyes, you will *never* believe what I saw! Two fish sticks. Ugh. It hadn't worked. Every single day of that week, I prayed for a miracle to happen. For something *absolutely wild* to happen. But nothing happened. I kept praying for crazy stuff like that to happen, but I went to bed disappointed every night.

"Mrs. Sullivan?" I asked her that morning in Sunday school.

"Yes, Carlos?" she replied.

"I tried to pray for a miracle like the fish one all week," I said. "But nothing ever happened. Am I not praying hard enough?"

All my friends, the flexible ones on the floor around me, started giggling. I remember feeling embarrassed and annoyed. Didn't they think this whole thing was crazy like I did? Didn't they want to figure out how to do all the wild stuff Jesus and the disciples did? Mrs. Sullivan saved my spiraling mind.

"Carlos, maybe this story will help you," she said.

Mrs. Sullivan placed the cutouts of Jesus's disciples on the flannel board and began to tell us a story about how sad they were after Jesus was crucified. "They were obviously sad," she said. "Their best friend on the planet had just been killed. They didn't know what to do."

Then she placed a cutout of a woman on the other end of the board. "This is Mary Magdalene. She was the very first person who saw Jesus after He rose again." Then she placed the cutout of Jesus on the board next to Mary. I hadn't seen this version of Jesus on the board before. He appeared almost . . . *shiny.*

She went on to tell us the Bible story for that day—about Jesus's appearing to His disciples after the worst day of their lives. Mrs. Sullivan was right; this story was about to change everything for me. Imagine the flannel board as I share this story from Mark 16.

Jesus asked Mary to go and tell the disciples that He was alive! But there was one major problem; they didn't believe her. Nope. They weren't having it. Let's be honest for a second. I don't know if I would have believed her either. I mean, He had just been crucified! But what I love about this story is that when Jesus showed up to see His friends and disciples again, He let them have it. He laid into them!

I love the way this interaction is set up: "Afterward he appeared to the eleven themselves as they were reclining at table" (verse 14, ESV). I can imagine the conversation that was happening around the table, especially because it says they were reclining. The Greek word *anakeimai* means to recline as a corpse or at a meal.[1] Obviously, I didn't look up the Greek word when I was eight, but I have since learned the meaning, and I now have a new way I want to eat.

So imagine for a second, the eleven disciples totally relaxing around the table. Arguing about whether Mary is crazy or not. It sounds like they were just chillin'. Then Jesus showed up and the very first thing He said to them wasn't, "Hey, guys, it's Me! Can you believe it? I pulled it off! I'M ALIVE!" Nope. That's not how it went down.

The first thing Jesus said to His disciples after He rose again was a little more harsh. The Scriptures say, "He rebuked them for their lack of faith and their stubborn refusal to believe those who had seen him after he had risen" (verse 14). Sounds to me like they got a pretty harsh tongue-lashing. Almost as if Jesus was trying to say that things were about to get crazy and if they were all in, they'd better buckle up. Because there was going to be no more room for doubt.

Then, after they were probably feeling super guilty, Jesus went on to tell them the thing that my eight-year-old self had been waiting an entire week to hear. I just didn't know it yet.

He said to them, "Go into all the world and preach the gospel to all creation. Whoever believes and is baptized will be saved, but whoever does not believe will be condemned. And these signs will accompany those who believe: In my name they will drive out demons; they will speak in new tongues; they will pick up snakes with their hands; and when they drink deadly poison, it will not hurt them at all; they will place their hands on sick people, and they will get well."

After the Lord Jesus had spoken to them, he was taken up into heaven and he sat at the right hand of God. Then the disciples went out and preached everywhere, and the Lord worked with them and confirmed his word by the signs that accompanied it. (verses 15–20)

After Mrs. Sullivan finished the story, which I'm sure she told with a little less commentary than the way I just told it, she simply looked at me and smiled. I remember my heart was pounding and my mouth was hanging open.

Drive out demons? I thought. *Speak in new languages? Have superhuman powers? Heal people?* My eight-year-old mind was going wild. I was a disciple of Jesus! That meant this stuff was gonna happen to me! I realized in that moment why Mrs. Sullivan told me that the story would answer my questions. These miracles, these signs and wonders, and this wild faith? It wasn't meant to be a magic show. It was meant to change people's lives. It was meant to take people from weak . . . to WILD.

As an eight-year-old, I was ready to experience all that Jesus told His disciples they would experience. But then a funny thing happened. I grew up. I got older. My confidence slowly went from looking like the disciples' faith *after* Jesus's pep talk, which is called the Great Commission, to looking like the disciples' faith *before* the pep talk. As an adult, I began to find myself doubting all sorts of things about what Jesus said my life should look like.

Adult life and circumstances had kidnapped my childlike faith. Worry robbed my wonder. Anxiety robbed my amazement. For you, it may have been fear, doubt, or anger. The cause may be different, but the effect is the same. For me, it was unreal levels of anxiety. Before I knew it, I found myself like many of us in the church . . . with a small, boring faith. A mild faith.

But what if I told you that you don't have to stay here? What if I told you that a mild faith can blow up into a WILD faith? Will it take hard work? Yes. But here's the truth: you *can* wake up every single morning and sprint into a day filled with miracles, signs, and wonders. It's possible. Absolutely. It happened to me.

Let me show you what it's like to ENTER WILD.

PART I

ENTER REST

1

Gold Thrones

How abundant are the good things
    that you have stored up for those who fear you,
that you bestow in the sight of all,
    on those who take refuge in you.

PSALM 31:19

Is there more? Is there really, truly more to this Christian life than we have experienced? John 10:10 says this: "The thief comes only to steal and kill and destroy. I came that they may have life and have it abundantly" (ESV). This verse, THIS VERSE. This verse has confused more people than I can count. Is God's promise of life to the full real? Is His promise of abundant life an actual thing? Is His presence actually something we can tangibly enjoy on a daily basis? The simple answer is yes. The more complicated answer is also yes.

Look, the offer we have been given by God Himself is this: a life that is filled with heart-pumping, joy-releasing, victory-claiming, beauty-experiencing fullness! Now will all that be opposed? Of course. Opposed by what? Well, Scripture tells us there is an enemy in our midst who is not out to borrow, push, or upset. No, the Enemy is out to steal, kill, and destroy. But we have been given all the tools we need to fight and win.

You are reading the words of someone who is relatively fresh off the boat, having come from the land of sin management. The land of life hacks that lead to a "better faith." The land of self-help in Christendom. The land of learning how to become a Christian simply so we can get to heaven. Although those things are important and true, that's not all there is. And in the last few years, since I've been living in this new land of awe and wonder, I have seen more WILD than I saw in my previous forty. Maybe it's just because I finally started looking for it. Maybe it's because I was finally taught that it exists. I don't know why. But the proof is in the pudding. Things have gotten wild round these parts.

In my previous book, *Kill the Spider,* we went on a journey from death to life, from believing lies to believing truth. A spider is a lie that you have made an agreement with, and once you have broken up with that lie, you begin to step into this new life of abundance. Notice I say "begin." The truth is we all have many spiders and the process of killing them doesn't ever end. We will discuss this more in later chapters, but for now we just need to get to the place where we understand what this abundance can look like and that it is real.

How is it possible that John 10:10, a verse meant to give us freedom, has so confused us? It's not the scripture's fault. Obviously. Just reading it, taking it at its word, is so life giving. But it's been taught incorrectly. Much of the pain comes in misunderstanding the meaning of the word *abundance.* That is where so many Christians get tripped up. And I know why. It's the gold. The shiny, gaudy gold. At least it was for me.

Is the Blessing for Me?

When I was growing up, we often drove past the TBN (Trinity Broadcasting Network) headquarters in Costa Mesa, California, off the 55 Freeway. My family would drive by in our 1981 Buick Regal, and I would stare in absolute awe and wonder. Five-year-old me was enamored with the gaudiness of it all. If you haven't ever seen it, imagine for a second if you combined Caesars Palace in Las Vegas, the Taj Mahal in India, and Daddy Warbucks's mansion in the 1982 film version of *Annie*. Yep. That's exactly what it looked like. I was constantly looking for Punjab (Annie's rescuer) to be standing on one of the balconies as we drove by.

"Daddy? Who lives in there?" I once asked my dad.

"Oh, Carlitos. Nobody lives there. That's a Christian TV station," he responded.

A Christian TV station? My little mind would spin. We were Christians, but I didn't know any Christians who had digs like that. Maybe Christian movie stars? I mean, isn't that who worked there? Christian celebrities? Probably. And we were not that. My dad was the pastor of Primera Iglesia Bautista de Pico Rivera or First Bilingual Baptist Church in Pico Rivera, California. There was absolutely nothing about our lives that matched that place, at least from what I could see. I'd never seen the inside though. Maybe just the exterior was fancy.

"Dad? What does the inside look like?"

When we got home, he showed me. He turned on TBN. I think it was channel 56. Bill Gaither was singing "The King Is Coming" with a few other men in white suits, and there were lots of old people crying as they sang along. They were singing on gold microphones in front of gold columns and these *massive* red velvet chairs with gold trim. The floor was marble, and there were these two people sitting behind the quartet mouthing every single word.

"Who are they, Daddy?" I asked.

"They are like the pastors of the TV station, Carlitos." THEY WERE LIKE MY DAD! I can literally feel the emotion as I type, the hope and desire that began to creep into my chest. Was this sort of lavishness made for us too? Maybe we would have this one day. My dad was the pastor. He loved God. This had to be the goal. Right?

I started watching TBN when nobody else was around. The lady pastor, the woman with the big hair and all the makeup . . . she was so pretty and so confident. She would stare into the camera and say stuff that made me feel like God was on my side. Her words made me confident I would have all that Daddy Warbucks stuff, too, someday. I didn't necessarily know what "sow a seed" meant, but as a child I wanted to do that if it meant my familia would end up with all that swag.

Is this it? Is this what Jesus was talking about in John 10:10? This bougie life I saw on TBN? And if John 10:10 is for real, then why is life so insanely *hard*? You pray for that promotion, someone else gets it. You pour your blood, sweat, and tears into a dream, and it fails to turn out. You try counseling to fix your marriage, and your spouse doesn't want it as bad as you do. You are believing for physical healing; your symptoms get worse. And let's get to the crux of this book. You lean into your faith like you never have before, reading the Bible, praying every morning, going to church every week, listening only to Christian music—you are *doing it all right*—but it all seems to fall short of the promise. You hear sermons talking about freedom and abundant life, of peace that passes all understanding, but this stuff never seems to materialize for you. It seems like an unattainable goal, and life is just so unrelenting. How can we live the truth of God's promise while on this side of heaven? It seems impossible.

5.4 Percent Abundance

My daughter Sohaila has struggled with eczema her entire life. And it's not the type of eczema that you rub some steroid cream on and it gets better. No, it's brutal. She can't sweat or it feels like her skin is on fire. This means she can't run, jump, dance, or even worship in church with abandon. She wants to jump and spin while she sings praises to God, but *it hurts*. It's been brutal to watch her suffer with it. We have tried everything. Allergy tests. Diet restrictions. All the creams. Different doctors. Eastern medicine. All of it. We have prayed until we were out of words and fasted for her healing. We have broken agreements she may have made with sickness—taking lies she might've believed from the Enemy, such as "Eczema can never be cured," and replacing them with truths from God and His Word, such as God "heals all my diseases" (Psalm 103:3, NLT).

At one point in her journey, I felt like God told me Sohaila was going to be healed in 2016. I actually wrote it in my prayer journal. I thought God specifically said that her healing was coming that year. So I leaned into the hope I felt and started praying for her healing with more vigor than I had in the past. This was her year of freedom! Well, you can probably guess the end of this story. New Year's Eve 2016 came, and I began arguing with God. *Why hasn't it happened yet? Maybe when the clock strikes midnight, she will suddenly stop itching.* Well, not only did the itching not stop. That first week of the new year, she was more miserable than she had been in months.

My heart was destroyed. Did I not pray hard enough? Did I not hear God correctly? I was gutted. It felt almost like a death. Sure, it was the death of a dream, but it was a death nonetheless. *Has God abandoned us? Do I just need to accept it?*

Friends. Time after time, in event after event, we are being hard pressed. These months and years of trauma begin to take their toll on our belief in the second half of John 10:10. We find it easier to believe in the part that says, "I came that they may have life." But maybe Jesus was talking only about eternal life, saying that things will get better when we get to heaven. Because surely He wasn't talking about right here, right now. I mean, life gets SO HARD. And we just ignore those last words about abundance and fullness as our confidence in them begins to erode.

Either we are not living this Christian life correctly, or God's promises are for someone else, not us. These are the agreements we end up making. But every time I open my Bible, I see these promises. It seems clear that Jesus actually, truly believes we can live a life *fully alive.*

Then Jesus declared, "I am the bread of life. Whoever comes to
me will never go hungry, and whoever believes in me will never
be thirsty." (John 6:35)

Whoever believes in me . . . rivers of living water will flow from
within them. (John 7:38)

Above all else, guard your heart,
    for everything you do flows from it. (Proverbs 4:23)

Again, people have taken this word *life* and reduced it to eternal life,
meaning we will get all this abundance and blessing when we die and go
to heaven. It's as if they're saying, "Abundance is coming! You may catch a
glimpse of it here and there. But you are gonna have to wait until you get
to heaven to actually, truly experience life to the full."

And that teaching makes sense to most of us because that is just how
life has turned out. We catch glimpses of abundant life—but only glimpses.
Take, for example, a typical family vacation to Disneyland, "The Happiest
Place on Earth." The day normally goes like this.

You wake up the kids and anticipation is through the roof. They have
been looking forward to this day for weeks, and it's finally here. So you pile
into the car and drive to the park. You have to wait thirty minutes to park
because it seems like every other human being on the planet decided to
come to Disneyland on the exact same day. After hearing, "When are we
going to park?" from the kids twenty times, you finally find a spot in Parking Lot Pluto 2. But you're still not at the park. You're still A MILLION MILES
from the park, and you now have to wait thirty more minutes with the
masses to squeeze into a special tram that finally takes you into the park.
It's okay. The anticipation is still winning. The music they are pumping
over the loudspeakers is soothing your soul. The Disney magic is still feeling like magic.

You finally get to the park; now you have to get the tickets. After taking out a second mortgage and selling your spouse's kidney and your soul, you have the tickets! Time to get in line to enter the park. Once you get in, you head straight toward everyone's favorite ride, the Jungle Cruise! You loved this ride as a kid and nostalgia tells you that your kids are going to love it too. The line for this ride is sixty-five minutes. Sixty-five minutes? Wow. But it's okay. You are at Disneyland! So you tough it out and finally make it onto the boat. The ride lasts five minutes. Halfway through the ride your eleven-year-old looks at you and says, "I'm bored." Talk about soul-crushing words.

"Well, what ride do you want to go on, Johnny boy?" you ask.

"I want to go on a roller coaster!" he shouts, so you head toward Space Mountain.

But your five-year-old is too little to ride, so you and your spouse split up and she heads toward a more age-appropriate ride. Walking up to Space Mountain with your eleven-year-old, you see that the wait time is 120 minutes. The line is TWO HOURS LONG? After you plead with your kid for several minutes to forget it, he still wants to wait in line, so you accept your fate. And you wait. Your phone battery is now at 15 percent, and you can't scroll Instagram enough times to make it interesting anymore. Two hours later you finally get on the ride. It's over in three minutes. Three minutes! But your eleven-year-old had a blast, so worth it! You exit the ride and meet up with your wife and exhausted kindergartner.

"Lunch?" she asks.

So you head over to the closest restaurant where you spend a hundred dollars on four hamburgers and fries. Really bad hamburgers at that. It's now two o'clock in the afternoon, and it's time for a parade! So you and the fam hurry over to Main Street, U.S.A. to watch the parade. There is zero shade and it's ninety degrees outside. Your five-year-old can't see, so you put her on your shoulders. The dad behind you starts cussing because now his kid can't see. But when Cinderella walks by, everything is worth it because your kid is shouting, "I see Sliperella! I see Sliperella!" And you don't correct her because it still warms your heart so much when she mispronounces Cinderella.

It's now three thirty, and you head to Pirates of the Caribbean because it's all inside and oh, my, you are about to have heatstroke. Seventy-five minutes later you exit that ride carrying your sleeping five-year-old and asking your eleven-year-old to please stop complaining about how his feet hurt because EVERYONE'S FEET HURT. You give your spouse the look. The look that says, *I know the park is open for about seven more hours, but can it be done? Can this please end?* To which she looks back with eyes that say *yes and amen.*

And with that . . . you exit "The Happiest Place on Earth," and while sitting on the tram, post a picture of you and the family in front of the Sleeping Beauty Castle along with #DisneyDreams.

There it is. The Dream Life. With 5.4 percent abundance. Exactly what we expect. The dream of what Disneyland could be for your family versus the reality of what Disneyland is. We get glimpses of glory in the midst of a rough day, so we chalk it up to "that's life" and go to sleep thanking God that we get to experience 5.4 percent abundance again tomorrow.

A Different Vision of Abundance

But what if it's not God's plan that we only catch glimpses of the best? What if you could go to Disneyland and have it turn out like my family's trip to Universal Studios last summer? Stay with me here.

We told the kids that when they all finished reading the Harry Potter books we would take them to Universal Studios in Florida to experience the Wizarding World of Harry Potter. The time had come. The road trip down to Orlando was exactly what I described in that Disney Nightmare montage. Long drive but HIGH EXPECTATIONS. There are two different

Harry Potter experiences at Universal Studios, based in two different parks. So if you want the full experience of Diagon Alley and Hogsmeade, you literally have to pay admission to both parks. And if you do pay both admission fees, you get to ride in the Hogwarts Express train from land to land. It's actually an incredible experience but, alas, one that we couldn't afford. From the start, we told the kids they could choose only one of the lands. Look at us. Already cutting their abundance in half before we even got there. The day before we planned to go to the park, I texted a pastor friend of mine named Josh in Orlando to see if we could meet for coffee. He asked why I was in town, and I told him we were going to the Wizarding World of Harry Potter at Universal Orlando.

"Have you guys bought tickets yet?" he asked nonchalantly.

"No. Do you know of a place that has a sweet deal? Because, man, it's expensive just to go to one park!" I replied.

"I can do a little better than that." He continued, "The VP of Universal Parks goes to my church. He has this thing called the gold pass that allows six people free entrance into all the parks and passage to the front of every line. So no waiting and no paying."

Cue all the tears and excitement. *Thank You, Jesus.*

I didn't tell the kids. They woke up ready to experience only half of what they wanted to experience but excited and grateful for the opportunity. Sounds a lot like us, huh? We know the Bible tells us we get life to the full, but what we really believe is that we'll experience only a little bit of that.

But what did our kids get instead?

They got to go to both worlds, ride the train between them, and ride every single ride in both Universal Studios and Universal's Islands of Adventure without waiting in line. They got to experience both parks with 100 percent abundance! Now did that create a perfect day? Was everything perfect? No! We still had to pay for the overpriced food. It was still super hot. We still had to walk for miles and miles. We were still in the park with thousands of people; we were just playing with a different set of rules. And it made dealing with the bad stuff so much easier.

Listen. I'm not building my doctoral dissertation with this analogy, but you get the point. You are with me. I know you are. We can live in this world and not be of it. We can exist in the chaos of our lives while simultaneously taking advantage of the incredible GOLD PASS God has given us. With Him, we have direct access to the front of the line. We don't have to wait. We get to have an incredible existence in this broken world, an experience that so many people are missing out on.

You. Don't. Have. To. Stop. Halfway. To. Abundance.

You don't have to settle.

In John 10:10, the Greek word for this life filled with abundance or life to the full is *zóé*. Zóé simply means "life," but here it is used to mean something special: a new, special kind of life. The abundant life of the Spirit. It is a spiritual power, sustenance, strength, energy, force.[2] It is literally the radiant life of God given to us! And here's the thing. The reason you need it is because you are going to go through a great deal of trials and hardships in this life. You *need* zóé, that powerful force that comes from having the life of Jesus *in you,* because of all the other stuff this life brings. Because of the thief mentioned in the beginning of John 10! That thief who is here to steal, kill, and destroy. That guy? That guy can't touch your soul because of the zóé, the abundant life, the life to the full that is growing inside you.

You need the indistinguishable full life inside you because this world is *brutal.*

But, friends, we have mistakenly defined zóé or abundant life to mean a better job, more money, a fixed marriage, that house you've been dreaming about. No. Although those are great and fantastic things that God may give to us, those are *not* what John 10:10 is referring to. We have to switch our definition to mean abundance *no matter your job.* Abundance *no matter how much money you have.* Abundance *no matter your marital status.* Abundance *no matter your living conditions.*

What does Jesus mean when He speaks of abundant life? It's clearly not a nice little life.

Abundance has nothing to do with accumulating things and everything to do with accessing the King. When you start seeing John 10:10 through that lens, you realize that abundant life—life to the full—is available even in our darkest hours. Even when the test results come back positive. Even when you are two months into being unemployed. Even when your spouse has an affair and you don't think you can ever trust again.

How do we get there?

It's closer than you think. Let's dive in.

REFLECT AND PRACTICE

Be sure to write down your answers. We are going to use them to plug into the prayer you will find at the end of each part division of this book.

1. When you hear the phrase *abundant life* in a religious context, what sorts of lies does it produce about your life?

   It is unrealistic & unobtainable - "Abundant life" feels like religious jargon

2. In what parts of your life would you love to experience life to the full or life abundantly?

   Spiritually - particularly in worship. Relationally c̄ a partner & c̄ my family

3. In what parts of your life do you currently see evidence of this abundance? *I have hope & I enjoy decent relationships c̄ my kids*

2

Losing Our Minds

Thou hast made us for thyself, O Lord, and our heart
is restless until it finds its rest in thee.

SAINT AUGUSTINE OF HIPPO

Three miles an hour. Three. Miles. An. Hour. If I told you I was going
to sell you something that has an average speed of three miles an hour,
would you buy it? Who in their right mind would want to invest in anything with an average speed of only three miles an hour? Not our society.
Not this generation. We are constantly striving for bigger, better, faster.
But guess what?

You, my friend, walk an average of three miles an hour. That's you.
This is the speed at which we were designed to move.

What if—go with me here—the way we can finally find this wild
season of faith that so many of us didn't even know existed is not by speed-
ing up but by slowing down?

You see, the first step in this journey toward a WILD FAITH filled with
abundance and peace is going to seem counterintuitive. What if the way

we catch up with God is actually by slowing down? I believe this is the first step.

We will call it Entering Rest.

Rest has almost become a bad word in our society. Rest has been undeservedly linked with laziness. But that couldn't be further from the truth. Rest actually leads to increased energy, creativity, and awareness.[3] And this isn't just true in our physical lives. It's also true in our spiritual lives. Rest begets revival. Show me one single revival that didn't begin with someone hearing from God. We have to hear from Him. And the only way to truly begin to hear Him more is to lower the volume of life. Lower the volume of life, and the volume of God's voice goes up. Lower the volume of life; watch revival happen.

But the volume of life isn't going down, is it? Most of us have given in to the idea that it's never going to slow down or quiet down.

I'm fairly certain the human soul was never meant to bear the weight it currently bears. I mean, we are majestic creations! God created us with the capacity to bear massive amounts of emotional, spiritual, and physical pain. But I'm not talking about that alone.

I'm talking about the weight of EVERYTHING.

What I'm about to say is going to seem like the complete opposite of everything I have ever been about. And guess what? That's okay. Because with every white hair that has popped up in this beard of mine, I have grown in wisdom. Just call me Mexican Gandalf.

I believe we have too much access to other people's stories.

It used to be that in order to carry the burden of another person's story, you had to be there in person or call on a landline. You had to actually be *present* and *available* to partake in that person's story.

For centuries prior to the telephone, letters were the only means of being invited into someone else's story if you weren't actually there. That is how a story was shared and shouldered.

Now? We have instant access to hundreds, or even thousands, of stories at any given moment. Devastating stories. Exciting stories. Intriguing stories. Happy stories. Heartbreaking stories.

What I'm struggling with recently is this simple question: Were our souls designed to carry that?

In my previous book, *Kill the Spider,* I talked about how we use social media to medicate lies we believe about ourselves. But I'm not talking about the medicating here. No. This is something different.

There was a study done in 2010 showing that "every two days we create as much information as we did from the dawn of civilization up until 2003."[4] We are exposed to as much information in a day as our ancestors encountered in a lifetime. A few years ago, a study found that the average American spent more than 608 minutes a day consuming some form of media. That number continues to go up.[5]

Friends. We were "fearfully and wonderfully made" (Psalm 139:14).

We are so adaptable.

But as technology changes and moves forward at lightning speed, I think we all know in our hearts that our souls were not created for this.

Just like Adam and Eve in the garden, we were created for communion with God and each other.

But I believe we should be doing life at a fraction of our current pace. So what do we do?

BURN ALL THE PHONES!

Ha ha! Of course not. But I do think we must be intentional about how much we consume and how many stories we shoulder.

The even heavier question is this: Can we truly hear God when we are listening to so many others?

The Power of Rest

In 2014, my friend Brad invited me on a fly-fishing trip to Montana. I immediately rejected said invitation. Why? Well, because I'm a half-black and half-Mexican man born in East LA and my people, we don't really do that. Fly-fish.

I remember being forced to watch *A River Runs Through It* on a date years ago. I fell asleep in the first thirty-second scene as Brad Pitt slowly let that line fly back and forth behind and in front of him. Fly-fishing in Montana did not sound even remotely appealing to me. Even less appealing was the simple fact that the place we were going had *zero* cell service and no television signal. And the NBA playoffs were that week as well. Nope. Not gonna happen.

Also, no way was I going to touch a fish.

After my initial rejection of Brad's invitation, he texted me back: "Carlos. I know you said no. But will you do me a favor and trust me? Just come out for a few days. Trust me. You need it."

I need it? What in the world did that mean? What I needed to do was finish the 1,234,332 things I had on my to-do list. I definitely didn't need to fly to Montana for a week of fishing.

However, I felt a nudge in my spirit to go. So I went. Two weeks after turning down the invitation, I found myself landing in Billings, Montana.

For any of you who have ever been to Billings . . . it wasn't what I imagined Montana would look like. It looked more like Montana had up and moved and left Billings to fend for itself. I had envisioned mountains yet I was in the desert. A large man with a shaved head and a tattoo of a spider web covering his entire skull picked me up at the airport. His name was Timmy.

"Welcome to Montana, Carlos! You are gonna love it," he shouted when he met me at baggage claim.

I was already wishing I had stayed in Nashville. This was going to be miserable.

The next morning, we took casting lessons on the front lawn of our lodge. I was horrible. I looked like I was having some sort of seizure every time I tried to find the rhythm of the cast. It was as funny as you are imagining. *Why would anyone enjoy doing this?* I thought, dreading eight hours on a drift boat.

"Carlos?" asked a nineteen-year-old Montana-looking kid who had snuck up on me.

"Yeah, that's me."

"You're gonna be in my boat. Let's do this!" he said and told me his name was Brennan.

Brennan and I made our way to the river's edge with the boat. Within minutes, we were drifting down the Bighorn River and he had me casting off the left side of the boat.

"Now, Carlos, you are trying to trick the trout into thinking the feathers on the end of that fly line are a bug that has landed on top of the water. So do exactly what I tell you, and you are going to catch some fish," Brennan said confidently.

I remember the next few moments as if they happened in slow motion.

I was watching the fly Brennan had tied float down the river next to the boat. I saw a flash of light a few feet under the fly . . .

"There's a fish! Wait for it . . . Wait for it . . ." Brennan whispered, as if the fish could somehow hear him. I saw the silver flash again, this time a little closer to the surface. My heart was actually beginning to race. My eyes opened wider . . .

Then it happened. Again. I saw a trout rise up out of the water and open its mouth. I watched it suck down that fly and then disappear under the water.

"Set the hook! Set the hook!" Brennan yelled.

So I did. I lifted my rod tip up and the fight was on.

"Keep the rod tip up! Keep it up!"

This fish came jumping about five feet out of the water. It was pulling out line as I was trying to reel it in. After about forty-five seconds, I had reeled it close enough to the boat that Brennan could grab the net and dig down into the water. He scooped up a fifteen-inch rainbow trout and pulled it out of the net. It was absolutely beautiful. Stunning actually.

"You wanna hold it?" he asked.

"Aw, no way, man. I don't like the way fish feel," I replied.

"No way. You have to hold it! Then you can put it back. C'mon, man. It's your first fish!" he said.

It's true. I had never caught a fish before. So I clumsily held that trout and smiled for the camera. My heart was still pounding.

"Woo-hoo!" I screamed as I released it back into the water. "That wasn't fishing," I declared to Brennan. "That was hunting. That was amazing! Can we do that again?" I asked.

And we did. For eight more hours. It was one of the greatest days of my life. And. I. Was. Fishing.

Around two o'clock that afternoon, I found myself standing waist-deep in a Montana river feeling more alive than I had in years. I was pulling trout out of the river at record pace. (My record.) I was spotting trout. Casting to the trout. Tricking the trout. Holding trout. And laughing and smiling more than I had in years. All because of trout.

I had become a version of myself I didn't even know existed. I was a full-blown Rednexican. But I think the single most important thing that happened in that moment was not simply that I felt ALIVE; it was that I found the space to hear from God in ways I hadn't before. While standing waist-deep in that river, I began hearing answers to prayers I had been praying for weeks. I lowered the volume of life, and the volume of God went up.

It's been four years since that fateful summer day. And I now fly-fish every single week. As I travel across the country, I find myself waist-deep in rivers and streams trying to hunt trout. This activity has become part of my DNA. Or perhaps it was already part of my DNA and I just didn't slow down enough to know.

In my REST, I found LIFE.

Oh, my friends, how my heart hopes the same for you. My hope is that you will slow down enough to hear God in ways you never could have imagined. That you'll Enter Rest and begin to hear Him so loudly. So clearly. This is possible. It is actually meant to be normal. But first you have to lower the volume of life.

Let's start there.

REFLECT AND PRACTICE

1. Try to recall some of those moments in your life when you experienced a sense of "perfect" or true abundance. Those moments when the heavens and earth seemed to align perfectly. Write what you remember of those moments.

   It was last year at a family gathering when even my ex was there; everyone was happy & at peace - the world felt right

2. In what areas of your life does the volume need lowering? Note those areas. *All I do is work, sleep & eat. I feel like I need to lower the volume of isolation.*

3

Be Still

Be still, and know that I am God.
I will be exalted among the nations,
I will be exalted in the earth!

PSALM 46:10, ESV

Remember how I mentioned worry robbing my wonder a few pages back? Little did I know when I was eight that by the time I was twenty-eight, this worry would have grown into something so much larger. And it would not be busyness that would begin to pull me out of it. No, it would be rest. When you feel like silence does more to increase your anxiety than it does to cool it down, then rest isn't the thing you want to try. But believe me when I say that it was only when I finally slowed down, pressed the pause button if you will, long enough to hear from God about the root cause of my anxiety that I began to find freedom. We will dive into exactly what that looked like in a few chapters. I'm guessing most of you reading this book are missing the pause button on your life. You've got rewind, fast-forward, and play down pat. But that pause button has been broken for a long time.

Although it's easy to blame technology and the twenty-four-hour news cycles for our inability to slow down enough to hear from God, this isn't just a problem we have begun to struggle with in the last decade. It's been happening for a hot few minutes . . . or a hot few centuries.

Let's rewind a few centuries back to the days of Moses so we can all realize we're not alone in our current stillness struggle. Moses was the OG when it came to hearing from God. He had some crazy direct access to God Himself, and he was always making people uncomfortable with all the stuff God was telling him. The Israelites *were not* into it on many occasions in the Bible. They were slaves to Pharaoh and the Egyptians for hundreds of years. Not just "go get me some water" kinda slaves. No, these ladies and gents were breaking stones 24/7. Their existence was not a happy one.

Cue God calling Moses to lead His people out of slavery. Cue God sending ten plagues to Egypt. Cue Pharaoh finally telling Moses to just take these people already. Cue Moses being a good listener and leading the Israelites out of Egypt. Cue Pharaoh freaking out when he realized what he had just done and ordering his army to go chase down the Israelites and bring them back. Cue the Israelites looking behind them and seeing the Egyptian army coming in hot and looking in front of them and seeing nothing but the Red Sea. Cue the moment of terror:

> When the Israelites saw the king and his army coming after them, they were very frightened and cried to the LORD for help. They said to Moses, "What have you done to us? Why did you bring us out of Egypt to die in the desert? There were plenty of graves for us in Egypt. We told you in Egypt, 'Let us alone; we will stay and serve the Egyptians.' Now we will die in the desert." (Exodus 14:10–12, NCV)

Let's stop here for a second. If the Israelites were ever in a position where they needed to hear from God, *now* was the time. Instead, they did what so many of us do . . . THEY LOST THEIR MINDS. Yep. I know none of us can relate. But here is where the special sauce comes in. Here is where I think Moses gives us, whether you're reading this book in 2020 or 3020, insight into something we need to hear. I think Moses's response to the Israelites when they were frozen with dread and not able to hear from God is incredibly current and timely.

Are you ready? Watch this . . . "Moses answered, 'Don't be afraid! Stand still and you will see the LORD save you today'" (verse 13, NCV).

Stand Still. STAND STILL. This was how they were about to get saved? By standing still? I can just imagine a forty-year-old woman standing in front of Moses, sighing with her hand on her hip, declaring, "I'm sorry, Mr. Prophet. This seems like the worst idea on the planet. There is a huge cloud of dust in the distance, created by the hooves of the charging stallions pulling the chariots filled with spear-wielding soldiers. Our impending doom is upon us. And you want us to just stand here and take it?" This would absolutely be my wife's reaction if I suggested the same. Luckily for the Israelites, it wasn't me standing before them; it was Moses, God's chosen one.

Still. Stillness. The Hebrew word here is *yatsab*, meaning "to set or station oneself, present oneself."[6] This was the secret. This was the challenge. Could the Israelites, despite the chaos surrounding them, stand still? That sounds more like us, doesn't it?

Friends. Guess what happened when they stood still? Many of you don't have to guess because you know. When they stood still, when they relaxed, when they stood still long enough for God to come in and work in ways only God can work . . . WILD HAPPENED. Wildness like only biblical wildness could happen.

In verse 16, God instructed Moses, "Raise your walking stick and hold it over the sea so that the sea will split and the people can cross it on dry land" (NCV).

Then what? Crazy. Out of this world. WILD.

> Then Moses held his hand over the sea. All that night the LORD drove back the sea with a strong east wind, making the sea become dry ground. The water was split, and the Israelites went through the sea on dry land, with a wall of water on their right and on their left. (verses 21–22, NCV)

When the Egyptian army went after them, the Lord snapped His fingers, and the water show was over. And so was the Egyptian army. (Nowhere in Scripture does it say what movement the Lord used to release the water, so don't email me telling me He didn't snap His fingers. I just like imagining God snapping them and saying "Bye, Felicia!" as He turned back to the Israelites.)

When the Israelites STOOD STILL, then STOPPED, they were led to their Promised Land.

I feel like I need to remind us that *this actually happened*. This is not a fairy tale. This is the kind of God we serve. He is capable. We serve a God who does the impossible.

Oh, friends—those of you who have been trying so hard to hustle your way to an intimate encounter with Jesus—what if it has nothing to do with hustle and everything to do with hesitation? What if the way to intimacy aligns with more stillness and fewer systems? I know it's hard. My first attempt at hearing God showed me I've lost the ability to stand still. Although I don't want to throw a blanket statement at you, we have all lost the ability to stand still. The good news is that it's not our fault. Well, not entirely. But the bad news is it is our fault if we let our addiction to the current pace of life eradicate our ability to hear from God. Because a chaotic life doesn't lead to Wild; it leads to weary.

I knew I needed to change a few things in order to begin this new way of living. I knew I was going to have to rearrange all sorts of things in my life. And I'm not talking about rearranging our methods. I'm talking about rearranging our motives. More on that later.

For now, this is the key question: How can you lower the volume of life so that the volume of God's voice goes up?

REFLECT AND PRACTICE

1. What part of your life is filled with the most chaos?

   My thought life & private world

2. If God were to ask you to stand still in the midst of that chaos, what emotions would fill you? Fear? Worry? Peace? Write these down.

   Fear, shame, hopelessness, anger & frustration

4

Daily Prayer

Rejoice in hope, be patient in tribulation,
be constant in prayer.

ROMANS 12:12, ESV

If you haven't made the connection yet, the entire point of Entering Rest is not to simply rest. No. The purpose of Entering Rest is to hear from God. We slow down so we can hear God. There are too many extra benefits to list, but they include joy, gratitude, peace, focus, and fullness, just to name a few. But the main purpose of this first step is hearing God because that is where WILD really begins. Do you remember the first time you tried to hear from God? If you grew up in the church, you may have heard that you needed to have a daily quiet time. I remember the pressure. Oh, the pressure. Thinking, *Maybe if I wake up early enough I will hear from God better.* And of course it needs to last at least thirty minutes. Because apparently God can't speak in less time than that!

However, there is some value in this approach. I believe spending time every single day praying and consecrating the day is vital. It's an opportunity to offer everything about your day to God. I have used the same daily prayer for the last five years, which I adapted from a few different sources. You can find this prayer ("My Daily Prayer") in the back of the book, although the daily practice is more important than the specific prayer you use. It's not magic. It's simply a way to set the tone for your day and be very specific in communicating with God.

Friends, our attention span has been hijacked by 280-character tweets and 15-second Instagram stories. Anything that takes longer than sixty seconds now seems to last an eternity. In almost the blink of an eye, we have forgotten how to pay attention. We no longer want to do things that take time. My wife, Heather, has recently begun gardening, and she's gotten really good at it. I tried to get into it with her, but guess what? You have to do all this backbreaking work, and you can't enjoy the harvest for *weeks*! That is basically torture in today's world. And the hard truth is, the crop MAY NOT EVEN PRODUCE if everything doesn't go right. So many variables are out of your hands. The weather. Bugs. Gophers. So, the joy can't come solely from the harvest. It has to come from the process.

In a similar way, I have found great joy and fulfillment in daily Scripture-based prayer. I pray the same prayer every day. Every. Single. Day. But in the beginning, it wasn't easy. It's still not easy, although it is such an integral part of my daily routine that I can't imagine *not* doing it. But when I first started, let's just say things didn't go so smoothly.

The Best of Intentions

Going to bed the night before, I had actual butterflies in my stomach. You know the ones you got as a kid trying to go to sleep on Christmas Eve? It took me forever to fall asleep. Why? Because I basically assumed I was going to wake up with a three-foot-long flowing beard on my face and a staff in my left hand as I stepped into this new world of hearing from God *all day, every day.* Moses, you've got some competition!

I set my alarm for five fifteen in the morning. Because the earlier you wake up, the louder God speaks, right? I had set the coffee maker to start brewing at 5:10 so that when I woke up, I would arise with the smell of Colombian liquid love to jolt me into consciousness.

And off to sleep I went.

When my alarm went off the next morning, I could feel the adrenaline pumping through my body as I sat up. *I'm about to hear from God!* I shuffled into the kitchen and over to the coffeepot. It was cold. And empty. The two-hundred-dollar brew-your-coffee-before-you-wake-up coffee maker had failed me. That's okay. Who needs coffee when you have the Holy Spirit?! I walked over to my sofa, sat down, and put my journal on the coffee table. I opened my Bible and set it next to my journal. The sun was just beginning to rise and peek through the window behind me. When I looked at the scene before me, it was magical. It definitely deserved to be captured. So I pulled out my phone and started taking pictures. Different angles. These were Insta-worthy in every sense of that made-up word. I took a few minutes to choose the perfect picture and then opened up Instagram to find the perfect filter. I mean the scene was already pretty epic, but man if I could layer one of those vintage seventies-looking filters on top of this photo? Boom! Found it: the Nashville filter. There is literally a filter on Instagram named after my city. There's no LA filter; there is no NYC filter. However, there *is* a Nashville filter. Cue "God's Plan" by Drake. I smacked that filter onto the photo and started thinking about the perfect caption (I actually looked back at my original Instagram post, so I would have this right). I had it!

> The sacrifice is worth it. When the alarm goes off at 5:15 a.m., it's not easy to rise and shine. But when we rise and shine . . . God will truly get the GLORY, GLORY. Friends I know that the snooze button is tempting. But just think how much farther you will be able to get in your relationship with Jesus if you rise before the sun to spend time with the SON.

Listen. If you can't appreciate the line from that old Sunday school classic "Rise and Shine," then either you are under thirty years old or you hate me. And the line about the sun and the Son? If they gave out Pulitzer Prizes for Instagram captions, I would be in the running. By the time I finished documenting the glorious scene, it was six thirty. Wow. An hour and fifteen minutes of being awake, and I hadn't even started the prayer yet. That's fine. I needed to capture that. Finally, I opened my journal and started praying the daily prayer aloud.

"Dear God, holy and victorious Trinity, I come to be restored in You, renewed in You, and brought back to receive Your love and Your life and all the grace and mercy I so desperately need . . ."

Bzzzzzzt. Bzzzzzzt.

Who in the world is texting me at six thirty in the morning? I looked down at my phone and saw two notifications on my screen. Somebody just liked and commented on my Instagram post about spending time with God. Sweet! Without hesitating, I picked up my phone and swiped up. *Whoa!* Someone left a comment telling me he or she was up spending time with God too! *That's so rad that there is an army of early risers getting our God time in together. That's inspiring.* I replied, saying we should see how many people we could get to wake up with the sun and do their quiet times with us. Our hashtag would be #BeatTheSunForTheSon. So I went ahead and edited my initial post with the new hashtag so people could get on board.

When I clicked my hashtag, I saw that someone had already claimed it! Ugh. Whatever. But who was this person? Wait a second. I knew the person. I mean I didn't *know* her, but I knew her. *I had no idea she was a Christian. That's weird.* She didn't seem like the type to wake up early to spend time with Jesus. A few clicks and several minutes later, I realized her hashtag meant waking up to work out so she would be healthier for her child. It made so much more sense now.

I looked back at the clock, and now it was seven o'clock. What in the world? *Focus, Carlos. This is ridiculous.* Okay, back to the prayer. I got through another two paragraphs, and my son, Losiah, walked out. His bedhead and rosy cheeks were too much. This kid is cute.

"Hey, buddy, come over here. Sit with Daddy. I'm spending some time with Jesus!"

He came over and sat next to me, put his head on my shoulder, and before I knew it, he was asleep. I just stared at him. My goodness, I love that kid. As I got another minute into the daily prayer, I noticed my eyes were heavy. Like I could barely keep them open. *I'll just cuddle with my kid on the sofa for ten minutes . . . just a catnap and then I'll feel better,* I thought. So I set the timer on my phone for ten minutes.

Ninety minutes later, I woke up to Heather saying, "Babe, didn't you have a meeting at nine?"

I leaped up, light headed, heart racing, and sprinted to get ready.

I. Am. A. Failure. How in the world did that happen? I woke up so early to spend time with Jesus, and I didn't even get 15 percent of the way through my daily prayer. But my Instagram post? By the time I woke up, it was already up to seventy-eight comments. People told me how hard it was for them to do this but that I was inspiring them.

Guys. This was real life in 2015. As I'm writing this in 2019, it's even more of a struggle. This was my first attempt at hearing from God while praying through my daily prayer. It could not have gone worse. I tried to get through the prayer two more times that day, with no success. I'm not saying God did not hear the words I actually did manage to pray, but my goal of a fifteen-minute consecration of my day to God did not happen. There were so many distractions. So many. In fact, the word *distraction* seems too soft. It feels like culture is assaulting us with information, more than our minds know what to do with. Life is so loud. Suddenly, the question isn't just, What is God going to say today? The question becomes, How am I even going to hear God today?

But Carlos? Daily prayer? That's how we are going to Enter Wild? It's the beginning, amigos. Trust me on this. When you start praying Scripture on a daily basis, you will begin to see mountains move. Why? Well, because you are praying Scripture over your day and the kingdom over which God has given you authority here on earth (see Genesis 1:26–28). Before things can get wild, you must slow down enough to invite the presence of God into your life.

This actually accomplishes a few things for us:

- *Daily prayer consecrates our day. Consecrate* is just a fancy way of saying dedicate. Say it. Consecrate. Don't you feel fancier already?
- *Daily prayer brings us back into fellowship with God the Father.* I don't know about you, but I can sometimes get to lunch feeling like the greatest follower of Christ on the planet, but then by the time bedtime rolls around, I'm as close to agnostic as I've ever been. These days take a toll on us. Praying Scripture is a great way to reset. Oswald Chambers wrote, "We tend to use prayer as a last resort, but God wants it to be our first line of defense."
- *Daily prayer slows us down.* Unless you are an Amish farmer living in the rolling hills of Pennsylvania, you need this. You need to slow down. We all need this.

If we base our faith on our day-to-day feelings as we live this roller-coaster of a life, we are going to end up chewed up and spit out. The job didn't work out. Our kids are a hot mess. Our marriage isn't what we dreamed it would be. The cancer came back. These things are bound to mess us up something fierce if we aren't bound to this truth: "God shows his love for us in that while we were still sinners, Christ died for us" (Romans 5:8, ESV). There is something important about declaring truths aloud in prayer, rather than just in our heads, on a daily basis.

Another essential on this journey to Enter Wild is a journal or notebook. Yes. Even for those of you who have never kept a journal before in your entire lives. This will be a place where you can write down all the things God is going to reveal to you during your prayer time. It doesn't have to be fancy. You can even keep a journal on your phone, although I prefer actual journals because you can see the tearstains. But please trust me when I say you need a journal for this part of the process.

Go ahead and pray now, either using the prayer in the back of the book or creating your own Scripture-based prayer. Pray slowly and with purpose. Pray again tomorrow morning. You can initiate the spiritual direction of your day. Your prayers don't have to be reactionary. Instead, you can be on the offense. You can step into your day knowing that you have called forth and commanded the kingdom of God to touch every facet of your life. We have the ability to enforce ALL THAT GOD HAS ALREADY PROVIDED FOR US.

Try it. Test It. Give it seven days. I have 100 percent confidence that this practice of praying every day will begin to open you up to abundance in ways you never dreamed.

REFLECT AND PRACTICE

1. List three hurdles you need to overcome in order to spend time with God daily. *Following / Creating a morning structure.*
Overcoming poor sleep
Letting go off perfection / all or nothing thinking

2. Look at your schedule and find a thirty-minute slot every day when you can have uninterrupted time with God.
In the morning 6:30-7am
In the afternoon after work
Before bed 09:30 - 10:00pm

5

I Finally Heard!

This is what the LORD says, he who made the earth,
the LORD who formed it and established it—the
LORD is his name: "Call to me and I will answer you
and tell you great and unsearchable things you do
not know."

JEREMIAH 33:2–3

It took a minute. Or more like 20,160 minutes, which is two weeks. Two weeks until I finally found a cadence that worked in my life and allowed me to make daily prayer a regular practice. Who knew slowing down would be so much work? But I did it. I finally slowed down enough to catch my first glimpse of WILD. It was such a small glimpse. But it was my first glimpse, the first time I interacted with God on purpose, not by accident, in my regular day-to-day routine. This is what Wild is made of.

Thinking back to this first moment, I remember how massive it felt back then. Now it seems so normal because my days are filled with awe and wonder, conversations with Holy Spirit, and personal direction from the God who makes the earth spin. Insert mind-blown emoji here. Guys. My current reality, the current space in which I exist, where I get to have my mind blown on a daily basis, all started on a beautiful spring morning.

It was a normal Tuesday morning. The kids were outside jumping on the trampoline. It was sometime after breakfast but before lunch. Miles Davis was playing on the record player, and Heather was sipping her coffee in the sunroom. Although the setting was picturesque, my soul was not at ease. I had been slowly praying through my daily prayer for several days, but my mind was a mess of anxiety. I remember thinking to myself as I walked past Heather on the blue sofa, *Maybe I'm doing something wrong. I'm praying this prayer every day, and I'm still riddled with anxiety.* I'd been working for years to find freedom from anxiety, and although I had overcome it in some areas, anxiety over my health still stuck. I'd been suffocating under the clench of its fists for decades. It came and went in spurts, but was always around, and this particular week had been worse than most. I'm certain I had spent 98.335 percent more time on WebMD than in the Word of God. So when I saw Heather snuggled up in the corner of the sunroom with the spring sunshine lighting her up like the most glorious Snapchat filter, I felt like God was mocking me rather than inviting me.

I'll just skip my prayer time today, I thought. *I'm not hearing God anyway.* There are a few sections of my daily prayer where I specifically ask God to show me things. So far, in the days I'd been trying this new practice, I'd gotten nothing. Zip. Nada. I hadn't heard a thing.

But as I walked past, Heather said, "Wanna pray the prayer together today?"

C'mon, God. I'm fine failing by myself, but I don't want to broadcast my inability to hear from You!

"Sure," I said, contradicting everything I just thought. I grabbed my journal and Bible and plopped down on the couch next to Heather.

"You okay?" she asked.

"Ugh. My heart is heavy," I replied. "I'm having a hard time with all this anxiety lately. I wish God would just show me the way out of it."

She smiled that simple smile she gives me when I'm in the battle, the one that says, *I don't fully understand, but I know you well enough to understand slightly.* Then, we began.

We spent the next thirty minutes in silence next to each other. I actually felt better the further through the prayer I got. When I came to the part where we crucify our pride, arrogance, unbelief, idolatry (and anything else we are currently struggling with), my belief that I would never be free from this health anxiety came RACING to the front of my mind. Like whoa, immediate tears. Immediate. That was weird. I don't normally cry like that unless I'm watching an episode of *This Is Us*.

So I wrote down in my journal, "I don't believe God can heal me of this anxiety." I kept praying. The further through the prayer I got, the louder that lie became and the more I felt the Enemy trying to inflate my unbelief. Then when I got to the part of the prayer where we command all foul and unclean spirits to the foot of the Cross . . . I literally stood up and yelled it. With tears rolling down my face and a good bit of snot building up in my nasal cavities, I YELLED IT. Woo-hoo! I was seriously feeling better already. Hope was rising in me. By this time, Heather was finished praying and was in the bathroom getting ready. She didn't get to witness my *Braveheart* moment. But that's okay. I was simply grateful she had invited me to pray. I was feeling stronger, and my anxiety had receded.

I flipped my journal to the next blank page and immediately got a lump in my throat. This was the part of my morning practice that felt the clumsiest, when I ask God what Bible passage He would like me to read. *Okay, here goes nothing . . .* I wrote in my journal, "Lord, what would You have me read in Scripture today?" And within half a nanosecond (that's really fast), I heard Matthew 14. Although I didn't actually hear an audible voice, that chapter immediately popped into my mind. Was it God? Was it the devil? Was it just me? Who knows? But I wrote it down anyway. I asked again what section of Scripture I should read, and again Matthew 14 came to mind. Well, I was hoping for a particular verse, not an entire chapter. After all, I had just spent thirty minutes in prayer.

Deep breath. Open Bible. Flip to Matthew 14.

Now the only thing different about this day was that I had picked up Heather's Bible instead of mine.

I know this Bible chapter well since I regularly preach on part of it, but I read it again. First, we learn about the death of John the Baptist. Then we have the story about Jesus feeding the five thousand. I remember realizing that when Jesus found out about His cousin's death, He went away to be alone and that's when the five thousand people followed Him. He was grieving when He used a few fish and loaves to feed a multitude. I remember thinking that was interesting, but not exactly revolutionary.

The next story in the chapter is about Jesus walking on water. Now this was a story I knew well, since I preach on it every time someone asks me to speak on my first book *Moment Maker*. Although it is a perfect example of a rescued moment, nothing fresh really grabbed me as I reread the story. I came to the end of the chapter and kind of shrugged my shoulders. I was hoping Matthew 14 would somehow mention anxiety or give me some nugget that would help me slay my health anxiety with one solid swing. But I found nothing of the sort. It was good to remember some of the truths in that chapter, but it wasn't as transformational as I had hoped.

I began to feel a sense of disappointment. But I pressed it down with the strength and newfound hope that had grown inside me as I prayed.

Right before I put the Bible down, I started looking at the verses Heather had underlined. This woman has turned her Bible into a work of art. Every page is filled with notes and highlights and things God is speaking to her. I'm not kidding when I tell you she sometimes writes paragraphs in the margins of her Bible. Strangely, her words were noticeably absent on this page. This page had nothing. Until I looked at the top of the page where one word was scribbled. She had written one single word with a hand-drawn arrow from the end of the word pointing to verse 30: "But when he saw the wind, he was afraid and, beginning to sink, cried out, 'Lord, save me!'"

Heather had circled that verse and attached it to the one word she had scribbled in the top margin. One word my wife had written on that entire page. I don't even need to tell you what the word is, do I? You know what word it was. *Anxiety.* RIGHT THERE AT THE TOP OF THE PAGE. I had just asked God to give me some insight that would calm my anxiety. Even though praying and reading Scripture was helping, I was looking for that specific word. Little did I know I was supposed to be looking in the margin! I love that this wasn't even an actual scripture that I was led to that gave me peace from anxiety. It was God saying, "I see you. I'm here."

"Heather! HEATHER!" I yelled. I sprinted to the bathroom where she was doing her makeup and started talking a thousand miles an hour. (I need you to read this next part at a thousand miles per hour.)

"Babe! You're never going to believe this! You know how I was praying about my anxiety? You know how bad it's been lately and it's basically all I've been able to think about? Well, as I was praying, I started to feel some of it leave. Like, I felt the Lord lifting it right off of me! Right when I asked Him to, He did! It was soooo good! But that wasn't good enough, so I kept going and asked God what He wanted me to read, and I heard Matthew 14, and I hoped that there would be a verse in there specifically speaking to my anxiety, and well, there was kinda but not really but sort of. Anyway, I read all of Matthew 14, and I was encouraged but didn't really find anything about anxiety."

"Babe. Slow down. I'm not going anywhere," she joked.

But the truth was I was freaking out. "Heather! The word *anxiety* didn't appear anywhere in those verses. But guess what? GUESS WHAT? At the top of the page in your Bible, YOU WROTE THE WORD *anxiety.* I can't believe it! God actually SPOKE TO ME. He told me to read Matthew 14, and I'm so happy I could cry!"

She hugged me, tighter than normal, almost as if she wanted to feel me while I felt Him. I pulled away and immediately asked, "Have you written that word anywhere else in your Bible?" Like she would know. She simply shrugged her shoulders, and I sprinted out of the bathroom.

I spent the next ninety minutes flipping through every single page of her 1,263-page Bible. (In case you ever wanted to know how long it would take to do this, it's ninety-two minutes on the dot.) Examining every margin. Reading all her notes. Studying all her scribbles.

Not. One. Other. Time. Not another time had she written the word *anxiety* in her entire Bible. And here's the cherry on top. If I had picked up my red Bible instead of her black one, if I had picked up the Bible I had been reading every day prior, it wouldn't have had the word *anxiety* scribbled on the exact page God had prompted me to read. No. I found it only because it was her Bible and that particular chapter. My soul.

Friends, that day was just a glimpse into this world of Wild that was waiting for me. But it was a big enough glimpse for me to tell God, *I want all of that and some seconds, please.* If He was this available to speak to me, could it happen again tomorrow?

And here's the good news. His voice just kept getting louder and louder, clearer and clearer.

Yes, there have been seasons of silence. But even in those seasons, I don't doubt He's there because I've also experienced seasons of thunderous volume. Now, here's the deal. I know I have some of you on board. But many of you may be thinking, *Um, Carlos, that's a cute story. But that is what is called a . . . coincidence.* And I would agree 100 percent had this not become a daily occurrence in my life. It stops being a coincidence after the seventh day in a row of God speaking.

Actually, it stopped being a coincidence when we made a decision to believe that a man who was fully God walked the earth two thousand years ago to proclaim this insane good news, then was murdered and buried and rose again, only to tell us an invisible Spirit would take His place on planet Earth to guide us on a daily basis.

If you believe that—and if you call yourself a Christian, you believe that—then you kind of have to let go of the whole coincidence explanation. There's no more room for that. Sorry. What you already believe about your faith is much crazier than my story about the word *anxiety* showing up in the margins of my wife's Bible. You are *already* wired for WILD. It's literally a thin veil away. You just have to walk through the veil.

And walk through it you will. Like right now. This is what I would love for you to do. When you get done with this chapter, go find your journal, pray the daily prayer (or another prayer of your choosing), and do this simple exercise. Ask God this specific question: "Lord, what would You have me read today?" That's it. Nothing complicated. The reason we start with Scripture is that it is *truth*, not *feeling*. So we know that we are just dealing with truth here. Let's not start this Enter Rest season with something complicated or overwhelming like, *God, should I quit my job tomorrow?* No. Practice makes perfect. Let's start small.

Where in the Word of God is He leading you? Read it. Meditate on it. And then maybe, just maybe, you will stand up and sprint to find the first person you see because it's starting to happen. WILD. It's actually beginning to happen.

REFLECT AND PRACTICE

1. What did it feel like to ask God a specific question and then wait to hear from Him? Was it awkward? Normal? Freeing?

   In the past it's been amazing to ask & hear. But I am filled c̄ self-doubt, making it difficult to trust I am actually hearing from God.

2. What scripture did you hear or feel led to read?

John 10:10 about the thief coming to lie, kill & destroy.

3. If you didn't feel or hear anything, that's okay. Try again
   tomorrow. Don't stop asking. And don't edit what you hear
   when you do!

6

Get Specific

In every situation, by prayer and petition, with
thanksgiving, present your requests to God.

PHILIPPIANS 4:6

The purpose of Entering Rest isn't to relax . . . or as my Mexican
mother so wonderfully used to mess up this phrase, "Take a chill-out tab-
let!" Remember the Israelites. They didn't need to stand still so that they
could lay out their beach towels on the shore of the Red Sea. No. They
needed to stand still in order to *hear* from God so they could receive all
that God had promised them. That is why we Enter Rest. Because it allows
us to hear the voice of God Himself, which will inevitably lead us into
abundance. We aren't looking for a vacation here; we are looking for direction. The goal is to mature into the person God wants you to be so that you
can thrive inside the abundant life He has promised.

So let's get super practical for a few minutes.

We've covered the basic steps of Entering Rest: praying daily, using a
journal to write your questions and God's answers, and asking the Holy

Spirit which scriptures you should read. If you did just those things every day the rest of your life, I believe you would live in the fullness and abundance God has planned for you. However, I also believe we have an opportunity for a much more intimate conversational relationship with the Holy Spirit, by taking one additional step. It is simple and it's the final step in Entering Rest. Ready? Two words: get specific.

Yes. Get specific. This is the piece that, for some reason, many Christians miss. Or maybe they don't miss it at all. Maybe they are just afraid to try. Why in the world would a God-fearing lover of God not want to ask God to meet his precise and practical needs? I know why. It's the reason I avoided making specific requests for most of my life. Ultimately, I was scared that if I got specific and He didn't give me a specific answer, then maybe, just maybe, He didn't really exist.

Now, I know that may be an extreme stretch for some of you. Perhaps you are in a place in your faith where you have few doubts about God. That's fantastic! But I'm assuming more than a few of you have these fears regularly. *What if I ask Him a detailed question and I don't get an exact answer? What if I ask and He doesn't answer at all?* That road has led some of the most faithful Christians to massive crises of faith. Unanswered prayers can drive even the most committed believers to doubt. For instance, two people ask God for healing but only one recovers. So we spread our prayers as wide as we can; we cast a superwide net when we pray so that whatever happens, we can say He answered. I get it. Developing the habit of asking for specific things is a scary endeavor. But I believe God always answers, although not necessarily in the way we had hoped. Friends, God is interested in our growth and maturity. He wants to give us our hearts' desires, while continuing to mature us in Him. Our desires don't always align with His desires, but that doesn't mean we can't ask for them. If we ask and He answers, but the answer wasn't what we had hoped for, He still spoke and our faith gets stronger. Let me show you what I mean.

Warring Priorities

A few months after my Enter Rest rhythm started to click, I found myself back on a tour bus. I was speaking with Bethel Music on its Worship Nights tour. Toward the end of our two-week run, I found myself in a coffee shop somewhere in middle America counting down the hours until I could go home. Fourteen nights sleeping in a bunk no bigger than a coffin will have you wishing all sorts of things. So there I was, one night away from being home, when I got a text message from my friend Justin. It was the sort of text from a close friend that I did not want to see at that moment. I just knew he was going to ask me for a favor I didn't want to give.

Hey, Carlos. Justin here. Hey, listen. So I have a huge favor to ask. I know this is last second but what are the chances you could come to our church Hope City this weekend and preach both services for Trish and me? We are both completely wiped from the adoption and just don't think we have it in us. We totally trust you with this and I'd really appreciate it if you could, but totally understand if you can't. Let me know. Thanks, man.

I just sat there, barely moving, looking at my phone. Ugh. I just wanted to go home and watch Netflix and do nothing, *nothing*, NOTHING. I was so road weary that I immediately started typing my reply, which was a horrible idea because of those dreaded bubbles that pop up on the other person's phone.

Justin! Hey, man! Bro, I would love nothing more than to help you guys out but to be honest, I've been gone from home for fourteen days and will have only one day at home before coming up to Indy. I think I'm supposed to say no this time only for my own sanity!

It's totally my bad for scheduling these two weeks of travel in a row. Literally any other weekend I'm free would be great! Heather has been running the house for two weeks and she needs me for a few days to help manage the kids and house. Hope you understand.

I'm so proud of you and Trish for the risk you took to rescue those siblings. Let me know if I can help you find someone! I know a few guys who would crush it!

Notice a few things here.

First, my use of exclamation points up top seems like such an Enneagram type nine thing to do. I'm such a peacekeeper. As if exclamation points are magically going to make someone feel better about the rejection he just received.

Second, I blamed myself for the rejection. I was basically telling Justin "It's not you; it's me." This strategy worked plenty of times in high school, so why not try it now?

Third, I totally threw Heather and the kids under the bus. If there is one thing I know in this season of life, it's that it's way more chaotic for Heather when I'm home than when I'm not. And honestly, when I'm home I'm not a huge help to her in running the house and taking care of the kids. I was really stretching for excuses at that point in the text.

Finally, I wrapped up that exclamation point sandwich with some positive Tony Robbins–style motivation sprinkled in at the end for good measure.

I hovered my thumb over the Send button, preparing to launch my thesis of a response . . . *Just hit Send, Carlos. Just hit Send.* My mind was racing for a few obvious reasons. Guilt, for one. I didn't want to disappoint Justin. Also, the fact was I hadn't actually talked to Heather. *Okay,* I decided, *I'll call Heather . . .*

I left the unsent text in the box and called Heather. "Hey, babe. So, I just got this text from Justin asking me to come preach this weekend, but obviously it's a bad idea because I've been gone for so long and I need some rest and you guys want me home, right?" I virtually vomited out the words.

To which I got a simple reply back: "Have you prayed about it?"

Um, way to throw that Jesus juke in, lovely. OF COURSE I HAVEN'T PRAYED ABOUT IT! Because what if God says go? "Um, well, I guess I haven't really asked God. I'll do that now and call you back. Love you." And I hung up.

What followed was a truly WILD interaction with God.

I pulled out my journal and opened it to the next blank page. I grabbed my pen and simply wrote this: "Jesus, am I supposed to preach at Hope City this weekend? Yes or no?" And I just sat there. I found it funny that I had actually written "Yes or no" underneath the question, just like I would have done in elementary school. As if Jesus would maybe just circle the answer and I wouldn't have to listen. But, alas, the answer didn't magically appear in my journal. I didn't feel any particular prompting in my spirit either. So I asked again. "Lord? Am I supposed to go? Yes or no?"

Asking yes or no questions is the *perfect* way to start when you are beginning this journey of conversational intimacy with Jesus. Let's not bet the farm with our prayers just yet. I wasn't asking God if I should sell my house. It was a simple question without a lot of emotional baggage hanging in the balance.

C'mon, Lord! Just say no already! I sat in silence for a few more seconds before I heard something, although it wasn't yes or no. It wasn't even maybe. I heard a Scripture verse. And when I heard it, I was certain IT WAS NOT GOD. Why? Because I heard John 3:16! That was the very first Bible verse I memorized when I was five years old, and the one that appears on a sign in every end zone of every football game on TV. Because of that, I nearly dismissed it. Surely God wouldn't answer my prayer by giving me that verse.

I was raised Southern Baptist, so the King James Version is what popped into my head: "For God so loved the world, that he gave his only begotten Son, that whosoever believeth in him should not perish, but have everlasting life." I kept praying and asking my specific question. Should I go and preach this weekend? I kept hearing John 3:16. And I kept editing the Holy Spirit.

We do this, don't we? How many times do we edit the Holy Spirit because we assume what we hear or sense can't be coming from Him. I assumed it wasn't Him not only because John 3:16 is one of the most over-used scriptures in the Bible, but also because . . . what did that verse have to do with my question? I mean, I wasn't giving my one and only son to Justin and Trish. *So what gives, Lord?* Then, out of nowhere, I heard *first.* First what?

Friends, again, when I talk about "hearing," I don't necessarily always mean an audible voice. In this instance, it was more of a prompting in my spirit. Not that we can't hear audibly; I just didn't in this moment.

I heard the word *first* again. *First? First what? First call him? First pray? First ask Heather? What in the world?* And then BOOM. First John. Not do something first. No. First John 3:16. *Maybe that's it!* There isn't just one John 3:16 in the Bible. There are actually four, including the gospel of John. Also, there are 1 John, 2 John, and 3 John. I heard the word *first. Okay, Lord. Let's see.*

So I turned to 1 John 3:16 in my Bible and slowly read the verse, taking in every word. Then I read the next verse. This is what the verses say:

> This is how we know what love is: Jesus Christ laid down his life
> for us. And we ought to lay down our lives for our brothers and
> sisters. If anyone has material possessions and sees a brother or
> sister in need but has no pity on them, how can the love of God
> be in that person?

I need us all to take a twenty-second dramatic pause. I need you to drop your jaw and not breathe for the first seven of those seconds. Now begin to breathe rapidly and look around quickly. Now stand up, put your hands on your head, and say slowly, "Oh. My. God."

Because that is exactly what I did. Wow. *Are you kidding me, Lord? Is this for real?*

Let's go ahead and unpack how crazy specific God's response was. I immediately thought of Justin when I read the line about laying down our lives for our brothers and sisters. Then, when I read about material possessions, I thought about the fact that I did have the time and ability to preach at Justin's church. I was convicted to shut down my quick and selfish refusal to help and instead respond in pity and compassion. It was clear that I needed to lay down my life—and my own selfish desires—in order to serve Justin.

Okay, God! I hear You, Lord! Please don't strike me down where I sit!

Friends, what did I say? We serve a specific God. A LASER-SPECIFIC God. And here's the truth. Even though God answered my question specifically, it wasn't necessarily in the way I initially wanted. But the second I heard this answer, it was blatantly obvious that the Lord wanted me to go preach. Suddenly, my excitement for the weekend ahead ramped up to a ten.

I reopened the messages app on my phone and deleted my unsent text to Justin. Instead I texted him this: "Man, Justin, how could I say no? I love you, man. I'll be there." My family and I ended up driving together to Indianapolis for a life-giving weekend.

He Still Speaks

Can you imagine with me for a second what would have happened had I just said no to Justin? I would have missed this experience of having my mind blown by God. Of course, we shouldn't say yes to every single opportunity that comes along. But we are supposed to ask God specifically about them all. Friends, I had never in my life read that verse in 1 John. God sent me that particular verse for that exact moment.

Amigos y amigas. HE STILL SPEAKS. He is speaking. He is waiting to take you deeper into relationship with Him if you would only stop praying in general terms and truly get specific. We don't serve a vague God. We serve a very specific God who knows the number of hairs on your head and can number the stars in the sky. I know you believe this, even if 99 percent of your prayers are unclear or imprecise. I know this because when trials hit, when hard times come, you get very specific with your prayers: "Dear Lord Jesus, I pray that tumor disappears in the name of Jesus."

But what if we did this all the time? What if our prayers went from vague to specific not just when we face problems but also in peaceful times? Can I tell you what will happen if you do this? Your confidence in God will grow so much that *nothing* can get in the way. The truth is we don't train for the battle while we're in the battle. We train before the battle begins. That way, when we find ourselves standing feet away from the Red Sea and an entire army of enemies is charging toward us, we can *stand still* with an impossible peace. We can be sure rescue is coming, knowing His voice will speak and the ocean will split.

By now, I'd gotten good at distinguishing between the voice of God and the voice of Carlitos. Things were good. But little did I know I was about to have my Red Sea moment. I would soon have to bet the whole farm that God would speak and come through.

Thank God I had Entered Rest.

Because I was about to Enter War . . .

REFLECT AND PRACTICE

1. What prayers have you been praying that are extremely vague? I pray in general for blessing, a partner & healing — but I also pray specifically

2. How can you edit those prayers to be more specific?

   I can pray for specific blessings & healing

3. Now pray those prayers.

   Lord. I pray for Your blessing on my efforts to improve my health.

4. Pray the prayer on page 61 as directed, using your answers from earlier chapters.

PAUSE AND PRAY

Father, Jesus, Holy Spirit,

I come to You now to bring myself back into conversation with You. I am asking specifically for You to begin to open my heart, mind, and ears to hear You again. I am seeking the abundant life that You spoke of in John 10:10, and I now renounce any lies I have believed about my ability to receive this abundant life. I renounce the lies that [insert any lies you wrote down at the end of chapter 1]. I pray that Your abundance begins to manifest itself in [insert the parts of life you wrote down at the end of chapter 1]. I thank You for the abundance I do see in my life. I thank You for being the One who brings all that to my life.

Holy Spirit, would You please reveal to me the parts of my life that are keeping me from hearing You? I surrender the chaotic part of my life to You: [insert the part you wrote down at the end of chapter 3]. I confess that this surrender is sometimes filled with [insert the negative emotions you wrote down at the end of chapter 3], and I bring the full work of the Cross against these feelings. Will You please begin to help me lower the volume of my life?

I thank You for the upcoming rest in my life. I thank You for the promise that You still do speak. Holy Spirit, I ask that You speak specifically to me in the coming days.

Thank You for being here for me and for speaking clearly.

In the name of Jesus, I pray. Amen.

PART II

ENTER
WAR

7

This Means War

The word of God is alive and active. Sharper than
any double-edged sword, it penetrates even to
dividing soul and spirit, joints and marrow; it
judges the thoughts and attitudes of the heart.

HEBREWS 4:12

When you read the Bible cover to cover, the common theme of the book is undeniable; it's war. The war between heaven and hell. This means you and I are living in the midst of a spiritual war. We have an enemy who wants to oppose absolutely everything good that we want in life. Knowing we are in a war, we should not ignore it. Can you imagine people in a war-torn country living their everyday lives, oblivious to the horror around them? No. They can't afford to forget that they are under threat. They are careful. They are strategic.

There is a distinct difference between spiritual warfare and worldly warfare. In spiritual warfare, we have the advantage of knowing we are going to WIN. We know that the Enemy will be defeated, even though he continues to fight. So let's start with this simple acknowledgment: we are at war.

I know I have mentioned my anxiety here and there. I've dropped hints as to how bad it can get. But the fact is that it was crippling. Entire vacations have been ruined. I have lost weeks when I attempted to sleep my fears and worries away. I spent months medicating my anxiety and numbing it with addictions. I feel like years passed in which I was not living at my full potential because I just didn't have it in me to fight this battle.

I'll never forget the week following my first panic attack when I was twenty-seven. After a few days of tests, my doctor told me to simply relax. Heather drove me to Fresno so we could stay with my parents while we figured out what we were going to do next. I had reached a point where I had zero capacity left to work. My job was to stand in front of people and sing, but I couldn't even back down my driveway without having a massive panic attack. Imagine the heart-pounding, sweat-inducing panic you feel when a cop pulls you over. Now, imagine that feeling continuing all day, every day. That's what I was experiencing, and I couldn't shut it off or control it. I was constantly shaking, I couldn't get my emotions stabilized, and I was suffering. When we got to Fresno, I remember walking through the front door of my parents' house, grabbing my mom, and sobbing uncontrollably. I whispered to her, "What has happened to me? Why isn't God answering my prayers?" *Why did anxiety have to be my thorn?*

I felt devastated and defeated. Every morning I woke up and saw the ceiling spinning above me. Immediately, my heart rate started climbing and my hands started shaking. It was a living hell. My mind was trapped in a prison of anxiousness. Not to mention all the messages from friends telling me to simply trust God. Yeah, great. Thanks.

A few days into our week in Fresno, Heather decided to spend the day with her family on their boat at Millerton Lake. "You should really try to come, Carlos," she told me.

"There's no trying, babe. I can barely walk to the car without melting down. I'm sorry. I don't know how to do this. I'm a prisoner in my own head," I told her.

I can only imagine what she was thinking at that point.

She was a young mom with an infant and a housebound mentally ill husband. This was not what she had signed up for. She left, and I moped around the house for a few hours. I picked up my guitar a few times and tried to sing a song, but it just sent me into another panic attack.

Around noon, something snapped inside me. I was walking past the bathroom mirror and my reflection caught me off guard. What I was feeling inside wasn't visible in my reflection. I stopped, walked up to the mirror, and stared at my face. I looked so normal. The panic I was feeling wasn't visible in my eyes.

I remember saying, "Get over this, Carlos." I repeated myself, louder this time. "Get over it, Carlos. Just get over it!" This continued until I finally screamed, "PULL IT TOGETHER!"

I tore out of the bathroom, grabbed the keys to our car, ran out of the house, and got in the car. I took five deep breaths and said to myself, "You can do this. You are strong enough."

I started the car, backed up, and started driving down the street. My heart was pounding, but I couldn't tell if it was because I was breaking out of my prison or from another panic attack. It was probably a little bit of both. I turned right out of my parents' subdivision and headed toward Millerton Lake to meet Heather and her family. I told myself, "This won't defeat you! You got this!" I was going to win! I was not going to let my panic win. I was going to muscle my way to healing.

About ten minutes down Highway 41, things started calming down. My breathing began to slow. My dizziness seemed to subside. IT WAS WORKING! Then, about a minute later, I found myself hunched over my steering wheel in the parking lot of a gas station sobbing. I had lost it again. Severe panic overcame me just as I was starting to feel some control over my situation. I couldn't make it. I called my dad to come get me. This was it. This was the last straw for me. All the determination and positive thinking in the world weren't going to get me out of this hole. I was going to need something more than hustle. I was going to need something HOLY.

I got an email the next morning from Sue, the prayer minister at the church where I worked. I've written about Sue before. She served on a volunteer basis, but she could pray the paint off the walls. In my last book, *Kill the Spider,* I described her like this: "She was about twenty-five years older than the rest of us. Every time she would come around me, I would feel peace like no other. You know those types of people, right? They just exude peace. When she would look me in the eye, she would pierce straight to my soul. . . . The first time I heard her pray, it was as if somebody placed an oxygen mask on me. I could breathe. It was mind blowing."[7]

That was Sue. In her email, she just had one request: "Carlos, can I pray for you this week? I want to come by the office and pray for your complete healing. Let me know when would be good."

My mouth dropped open when I read her message, not because it was a grand request. Actually, for the opposite reason: the request was so simple and sincere. I was also floored by her request because I realized that this was the first time anyone had specifically asked to *pray with me in person.* Of course, people were praying for me, but I realized that nobody had actually placed their hands on me and prayed for God to set me free. I'm guilty myself of rarely doing the praying *with* people after I've committed to pray *for* them, although I usually follow through with the prayer itself.

The other thing that shook me was Sue's brazen assumption that I could be healed of this anxiety through prayer. She actually said, "pray for your complete healing." Maybe she was crazier than I was.

A week later, I went to my office, still shaking and dizzy, heart still racing. I was exhausted. But there was Sue, smiling her peaceful smile that had healing properties of its own. "Let's pray, Carlos." And so she began.

She placed both her hands on my hands and began to pray. To be honest, I don't remember much of what she said. I remember only that her prayer was long, focused, and much more relaxed than I imagine one would be when praying in behalf of another person. She was definitely praying with authority and purpose. At one point, I remember she began to cry as she asked God specifically "to remove this burden from Carlos and place it on me. I can handle it, Lord. Please place some of it on my shoulders." Wow. I wouldn't wish what I was feeling on my worst enemy, and here was Sue, asking God to give it to her. I remember that after she prayed, Sue asked me to repeat the scripture she was going to read over me. "Carlos, you know the Word of God is living and active. It will literally make the Enemy flee. Let's use it, okay?"

She read the following verses, which she had personalized for my situation, and I repeated them. We were praying Scripture over my mind.

I am from God and have overcome him (Satan). The One who is in me is greater than the one who is in the world. (see 1 John 4:4)

I will fear no evil, for You are with me, Lord. Your rod and Your staff comfort me. (see Psalm 23:4)

I am far from oppression and fear will not come near me. (see Isaiah 54:14, ESV)

We went on and on. And can I tell you something? I honestly began to feel something lift, and Sue could tell. The anxiety didn't disappear entirely. But it began to lift in a way I had been begging God to do every waking moment for the previous two weeks.

"Carlos. Proverbs 4 says, 'Give attention to my words . . . for they are life to those who find them, and health to all their flesh'" (verses 20, 22, NKJV), Sue encouraged me.

This was the first time in over two weeks that I was speaking truth. I had been speaking destruction over my life since my initial panic attack. I started replaying some of my conversations . . .

"I'm useless now. I'm going to have this anxiety for the rest of my life."

"God has abandoned me."

"I'm so weak. I can't believe this happened to me. I can't even do my job anymore. I can't even find joy in my newborn daughter."

"I can't even drive without having a panic attack. My life is over."

"This is the worst. God, why won't You listen to me?"

Are you reading all that? It had been two weeks of me throwing all these words into the atmosphere of my life. Two weeks of nonstop self-pity. Yet it took only fifteen minutes of me throwing some truth back at those lies to get some relief. Just a bit. But relief nonetheless.

Now here is the incredible news. Sue kept praying for me, and I kept getting better. I started going to counseling. I improved some more. I started exercising. I continued to get better. I began taking 10 mg of Paxil a day. I was feeling more like my old self. Soon I was on stage again. I was leading while sitting on a stool because I would get dizzy if I stood up, but I was able to do what the Lord had created me to do once again. I was getting my life back and that was exciting.

But a funny thing happens when we start to get some relief from pain. Well, maybe it's not so funny. We forget what total healing and freedom feel like, and we stop going after total restoration because the little bit we have received is such a relief. This happens to the best of us. It happens like this:

- We are living our incredible lives.
- Pain strikes.
- We pray for relief.
- We get a little relief.
- We are happy with that small taste of healing, and we end up staying right there.

That is exactly what happened to me.

I actually never got back to the abundance I was experiencing before my panic and anxiety. When I got some relief, I was so grateful for the relief that I begged God never to let me go back to the full-blown episodes that had me in bondage. So my prayers became like little undercover bargains with God. *Lord, if You just never let me go back to that place, I'll be happy and never complain. I promise.*

That sounds crazy, doesn't it? Well, it sounds crazy until you have experienced a certain level of hell. And, friends, I had. Now I'd do anything to avoid going back. A medicated life of half abundance seemed like a reasonable trade. I wasn't miserable. I figured I'd just wait until heaven to experience all God has for us.

Amigos, JESUS DIDN'T DIE ON A CROSS SO WE CAN COPE! That is not the promise of the gospel. But how many times are we good with just half a healing? That was me. So I got it. I got my half a healing and lived with it for the next fifteen years of my life. Until two years ago, after my marriage had fallen apart and was put back together again. After seven days of experiential therapy and years of living what most would call a peaceful life. I was no longer having panic attacks and only had a little bit of anxiety, which was manageable.

I had grown so used to living this mild faith that I had no idea WILD existed. But before I could experience WILD, I was going to have to experience war. As I've said before, God is committed to our maturing. He does not want us to stay where we are. I thank God He didn't let me stay content with a mild, safe faith. But it took going back to something I hadn't experienced in fifteen years. It took Him waking me up by allowing me to face the very thing I had prayed I would never experience again.

The panic and anxiety that I had been managing?

It came back with a vengeance. Only this time the stakes were higher. And this time around I would be driven to find complete and total healing instead of partial healing. This time, I would not be content to simply find relief. I would be driven to find hope in areas where I didn't know I needed it. If I wanted to experience Wild, I was going to have to fight the war and navigate the darkness of a new spiral. I almost lost everything once again.

But God . . .

REFLECT AND PRACTICE

1. In the next day or two, find the time, even if it's just five minutes, to silence yourself and ask God this question: *In what area of my life am I currently just coping?*

   My private world – anxiety & panic attacks – loneliness

2. Look back at some of your recent prayers. How many of them are filled with negative life situations and lies from the enemy?

   Well – it's 2020 – so negative life situations abound. But I usually pray for blessing, prosperity & protection – so positive

8

Pray the Promise

Whatever God has promised gets stamped with
the Yes of Jesus. In him, this is what we preach
and pray, the great Amen, God's Yes and our
Yes together, gloriously evident. God affirms us,
making us a sure thing in Christ, putting his Yes
within us. By his Spirit he has stamped us with his
eternal pledge—a sure beginning of what he is
destined to complete.

2 CORINTHIANS 1:20–22, MSG

Now that we have Entered Rest and we are hearing from God, we are
going to start taking the next steps toward Entering Wild. But there is a
step in between Rest and Wild. It's War. This may sound terrifying, but
the war we fight will lead us toward abundance because it is laced with the
hope of the Cross. When was the last time you heard someone define war
as hopeful? Most of us have never been in that situation. But that's because
most of us didn't grow up in a country where we were sold, beaten, or
marginalized in the most inhumane ways. But in fact people who live in

those places actually DREAM OF WAR. They dream of having an opportunity to confront and defeat their oppressors so that they can find freedom. That's the kind of war I'm talking about here, where there is hope because those in bondage imagine a world without oppression.

We can lean into the same hope knowing that our oppressor has already been defeated by the blood Jesus shed at the cross. But in order to fight a war, we need weapons. Our first and most powerful weapon is the truth of God's Word, "the sword of the Spirit" (Ephesians 6:17). The beautiful thing about this weapon is that you don't need to have a master's degree in hermeneutics in order to wield it. You don't have to live in a holy hermitage or a mountaintop monastery in order to access the power in the Word of God. No. You have access right now.

What I have learned since starting this journey is that the Word of God *is* actually living and active. It is sharper than a "double-edged sword" (Hebrews 4:12). I used to see the Bible as a resource for learning about God. I didn't necessarily see it as a weapon I can use against the plans and schemes of the Enemy. Recently, I realized something that absolutely transformed the way I pray. You may not believe me at first, but trust me. Ready?

When Jesus prayed, He NEVER PRAYED THE PROBLEM. It's true. If you read the Gospels closely and examine the way Jesus prayed, you'll realize He never prayed the problem. He ALWAYS PRAYED THE PROMISE.

There are many instances in Scripture where we read that Jesus was praying, but we have only a few instances where His exact prayers were recorded. In John 17, nearly the entire chapter is composed of Jesus praying. He prays that God would protect His disciples but doesn't specifically identify any threats. This is such a small shift, but it has a huge impact. This is what Jesus prayed:

> Holy Father, protect them by the power of your name, the name
> you gave me, so that they may be one as we are one. While I was

with them, I protected them and kept them safe by that name you gave me. None has been lost except the one doomed to destruction so that Scripture would be fulfilled.

I am coming to you now, but I say these things while I am still in the world, so that they may have the full measure of my joy within them. I have given them your word and the world has hated them, for they are not of the world any more than I am of the world. My prayer is not that you take them out of the world but that you protect them from the evil one. (verses 11–15)

How many times have we prayed for protection but it sounds more like this: "God, I'm terrified! Help me! I'm overwhelmed! I'm so scared! Protect me!" Are you seeing the distinction? In one desperate prayer, I just declared three things over myself: I am scared, I am terrified, and I am overwhelmed. This is what I'm talking about when I say that we tend to pray the problem. Instead of praying like that, I urge you to pray the promise. Jesus was reminding His heavenly Father of His promise to protect His children from the evil one. Instead of praying our problems, follow Jesus's lead and pray the promise.

Here's another example. Even in one of His most desperate prayers, Jesus again prayed the promise, "Father, if you are willing, take this cup from me; yet not my will, but yours be done" (Luke 22:42).

Mind blown. Earth shifted. My spiritual life was completely gutted. Why? Because I began to analyze my prayer life. I started looking through my old journals and realized the way I had been praying was the complete opposite of this approach. My prayers were filled with "Woe is me" instead of "Great is He." I was a professional at praying the problem rather than the promise. The more I researched Scripture, especially the life of Christ, the more I realized that we should be praying the promise, not the problem, in every situation. I'm not saying we have to ignore the hard circumstances in our lives. No. I'm talking about declaring the truth of God's promises over our trials and tragedies. PRAY THE PROMISE. If you recall the last chapter, that is exactly what Sue did for me. She led me in praying God's promises over my life.

Christianity is sometimes called the Great Confession because our faith hinges on our confession of faith in Jesus Christ.[8] But so many times in my life I have been held captive because I was believing and confessing the wrong things. What ends up happening when bad situations arise is we declare and actually begin to believe the words of the Enemy.

For instance, with my anxiety, my prayers would often sound like this: "Oh God, I can't do this anymore! I'm so filled with anxiety. I feel like I'm dying. I can't go on. Please help!" Because I was praying the problem, I got stuck in bondage. Instead, I should have been praying like this: "Father, I know this anxiety is not of You. So I declare that I will be free from this anxiety. If there is anything inside me that is not of You, remove it so I can stand in the fullness and perfection for which You created me."

The words we speak are so powerful. I understand that when we are in panic mode, it's hard to focus on the words we pray. But if we keep at it, it will become normal to pray the promise. Jesus taught this principle often in the Gospels. For instance:

Truly I tell you, if you have faith as small as a mustard seed, you can say to this mountain, "Move from here to there," and it will move. Nothing will be impossible for you. (Matthew 17:20)

Jesus called the crowd to him and said, "Listen and understand. What goes into someone's mouth does not defile them, but what comes out of their mouth, that is what defiles them." (Matthew 15:10–11)

Speak the promise first. Don't just think in your head about what you need; declare it with your mouth. This is what Jesus did on a daily basis.

He spoke things into being. He spoke to the winds and to the sea and ordered them to be calm. He spoke to the demons and commanded them to leave. He spoke to a fig tree and caused it to wither. He even spoke to the dead and raised them to life with His words.[9]

We can simply look at the life of Jesus and do likewise. The words we speak program our spirits. And remember, I'm not just talking about positive self-talk. Sure, that may be helpful, but it's not healing. Speaking positively about yourself or your situation feels good. It feels motivating. And it's not necessarily bad, but it won't bring you lasting freedom. I used to be a self-help guru. But while I still believe such tools and practices can give you glimpses of freedom, nothing but the blood of the Cross and the power of the Resurrection will bring true freedom.

Tony Robbins is so motivational. Gary Vaynerchuk has so many incredible ideas. Oprah Winfrey is so wise. Although their messages are truly inspiring, they can get you only so far in this spiritual war. When someone gets sick, when you are laid off without notice, when your marriage is crumbling, inspirational quotes aren't going to cut it. No. If you believe in the gospel of Jesus Christ, that's what you need to be speaking over your life. You are declaring healing in the name of Jesus and not in the name of any great and inspiring human. Remember, God's Word is LIVING AND ACTIVE. Our words are containers that carry either faith-building hope or faith-destroying fear.

As it says in Romans 10:17, "Faith comes by hearing, and hearing by the word of God" (NKJV). Our faith will grow so much faster when we hear ourselves quoting, speaking, and praying the Word of God. I'm telling you, you will receive and believe the truths of God's Word more readily when you hear yourself saying these truths instead of just hearing them from someone else. This is why it's so important to start here when Entering War. When you feel you are lacking, you can speak the truths of God's Word so that you will soon have abundance. When you are being defeated, you can pray the promises of God's Word so you will be victorious.

Doing this isn't just to make yourself feel good! This practice actually SHIFTS THE ATMOSPHERE in your life. I've seen this strategy transform my life in the last few years. It's mind blowing.

Witness the Shift

In the summer of 2018, I was on a book tour for my book *Kill the Spider.* If you follow me on Instagram, you got a first-row seat to witness some of the amazing adventures my family and I experienced on that tour. It's kinda my jam to let my followers see the good, the bad, and the in-between. But for those of you who aren't yet following me (What's wrong? Go do it already!), here's what went down.

Halfway through the summer, I was scheduled to go on a tour with a band. I would be presenting the gospel, and I was looking forward to it not only because it would be fun, but also because it was going to provide two months of income for my family. You see, this is my job. I write books, and then I talk about them. Since our income comes in seasons, budgeting can be a challenge. So I rely on booking a lot of speaking engagements to pay the bills. We've never missed a mortgage payment, and God has always kept my calendar full. But something happened that was going to test my belief in this whole "speak God's truth and watch Him come through" approach.

One week before the tour was scheduled to start, the whole thing was canceled. Two months of income literally vanished with one email. And I full-on freaked out, like hands on my head, mouth hanging wide open. If the tour had been canceled a few months out, no problem, I could have figured out a way to pay the bills. But it was due to start in just a week. And nobody is calling for my services a week out. People are calling to book me a year in advance. Cue the panic. We were out two months of income, and I now had nothing on the calendar for the next six weeks.

I walked out of the bedroom where I had received the news, and Losiah, my youngest, could tell something was definitely wrong.

"What's wrong, Daddy?" he asked.

"Oh, nothing, buddy. Just some business stuff," I replied, brushing off his question.

"What business stuff, Dad?" he continued.

"Nothing, buddy. It's all good. I'll figure it out," I said, a little more annoyed than I was the first time he asked.

"Like what will you figure out?"

Come on, kid. Can't I have my moment of panic without you injecting your eleven-year-old thoughts into it?

I almost lost it on him. I was stressed. I was panicked. I didn't know how we were going to find the money to live on for the next couple of months. But just as the Israelites needed to do in their freak-out moment, I needed to STAND STILL in this moment. I needed to HEAR from God about the battle plan He was setting up before me. Thank God I did stand still because my son was about to get a sin-filled tongue-lashing from his broken father.

I took a deep breath and then looked him in the eye. I said, "Buddy, you know that tour Dad was supposed to leave on next week?"

"Yeah, Dad," he replied.

"Well, I just found out that tour got canceled. And that's why I'm stressed. I don't know what to do. We won't have enough money to pay the bills! That's why I'm stressed. Because we are going to have no money."

First of all, do you see how I was reacting to the situation? My response was completely the opposite of everything I just shared in the paragraphs above. I was not doing this right. But thank God for kids, especially this one.

"Oh, that's okay, Dad. You will get the money." He said it so confidently.

"What are we going to do, buddy? Rob a bank?" I was half joking and half wondering if I could pull it off. I've seen *The Italian Job*.

"No, Dad! God's gonna give it to you. Have you asked Him for the money yet?"

"Well, actually, come to think of it, no. I haven't asked God for the money back yet."

Which was true. I'd spent the last hour trying to figure out how I was going to get the money back and preparing to call all my pastor friends to ask if I could come speak on an upcoming weekend. I had spent the last hour in a panic. But you know what I had *not* done yet? I hadn't asked God for the money. And let me tell you why. Because I didn't want to ask and risk Him not coming through. It was that simple. I didn't want to ask God to provide for us financially and be disappointed. We've talked before about this—why so many of us don't ask specific questions. We don't want to be let down.

"Okay, Dad. So let's ask right now."

Oh man. Now I was stuck. It's one thing to ask God for something this specific in private so you're let down privately when He doesn't answer. It's another thing entirely to invite your impressionable son to take part in this faith-wrestling match. "That's a good idea, buddy. I'll ask God later when I'm reading my Bible. Thanks, though."

"Are you too busy to ask now?"

Come on! This kid was going to be the end of me. *Okay, fine. You want to test God with me?* All right, I would ask. But I was honestly only asking for my kid. Probably 80 percent for him because I had only about 20 percent faith that God could pull it off. Just being honest here. I was so scared to ask with Losiah because I didn't want to introduce any sort of doubt into his faith.

"Aight, kid. Let's do this."

I grabbed my Bible and my journal that was filled with truths from God's Word and found a few scriptures that we could speak over our situation. I also had some Scripture-based truths that I read in times of need. We would declare God's abundance in our current lack. To add to my annoyance, Losiah seemed so matter of fact and confident that God was going to provide.

I began by praying, "Lord, thank You for always providing for our family, and thank You for providing for us in this upcoming season of need." That's it. That's literally all I could muster up to say because I doubted so hard. However, the beautiful thing about the Word of God is that even if you are doubting, it's still true. Even if you run out of fancy words to pray, the Word of God is filled with powerful words. So I began reading the following scripture-based statements out loud with Losiah.

Christ has redeemed me from the curse of the law. Christ has redeemed me from poverty. Christ has redeemed me from spiritual death. (see Galatians 3:13; Deuteronomy 28:1–14)

In exchange for poverty, He has given me wealth; instead of sickness, He has given me health; and for death, He has given me eternal life. (see 2 Corinthians 8:9; Isaiah 53:5–6; John 10:10)

It is true unto me according to the word of God. (see Psalm 119:25)

I delight myself in the Lord, and He gives me the desires of my heart. (see Psalm 37:4)

I have given and it is given to me in good measure, pressed down, shaken together, and running over. (see Luke 6:38)

With the measure I use, it is measured back to me. I sow bountifully; therefore I reap bountifully. I give cheerfully, and my God has made all grace abound toward me. I have all sufficiency in all things and abundance for every good work. (see 2 Corinthians 9:6–12)

There is no lack, for my God supplies all my needs according to the riches of His glory in Christ Jesus. (see Philippians 4:19)

The Lord is my Shepherd and I lack nothing. Jesus was made poor that I through His poverty might have abundance. He came that I may have life and have it more abundantly. (see Psalm 23:1–2; 2 Corinthians 8:9; John 10:10)

The Lord has pleasure in the prosperity of me, His servant, and Abraham's blessings are mine! (see Psalm 35:27; Galatians 3:14)

By the end of the truth-telling session, I felt amazing. I honestly believed more strongly than I had when I started reading. It's incredible how quickly speaking the Word of God over your life can change your attitude. And although that was fine, I really needed my bank account to be lifted.

"There you go, Dad. Can I play my Nintendo now?" Losiah was ready to move on to the next thing already.

And so was I. I walked over to my laptop and opened my email. I started typing out an email to some pastor friends I knew, asking them if they had any open Sundays I could fill in. But before I could hit Send, I felt like God said, *No. Don't send it. Not yet.* I realized if I did this, I would be taking this situation into my own hands. It felt a little silly at the time. But I sensed God saying, *You just trusted Me. Now really trust Me.* Ugh. Okay, fine.

Fast-forward six hours of stressing and finally relaxing in hour seven as I watched *Live PD.* I realized there were a lot of people in worse situations than me. However, it was never far from my mind that I hadn't had a booking in weeks, and if anyone did call, they would probably want me to speak nine months out.

I decided to give God a day. But then I would have to do something.

At eleven o'clock that night, I climbed in bed, plugged my phone into the charger, and hit Play on my sound machine app. I closed my eyes. Then suddenly I heard, *Bzzzzzzt Bzzzzzzt.* (BTW, that's how you spell it when your phone vibrates.) *Who's texting me so late?* I thought, not recognizing the number on the lock screen.

So I swiped up to unlock my phone and . . . hold on to your britches, ladies and gents . . . this is what it said:

> Hey Carlos, hope u are well bro. This is Jarrod Ingle. Got your
> number from Mike Foster. Wanted to reach out and see if you
> would be interested in speaking at my church the weekend of
> July 14–15? I know it may be a long shot since it is right around
> the corner. Bring the family and we'll cover it. We'd take great
> care of u. I know it's last second, so no worries if you can't.

I just sat there in complete silence, mouth hanging open, heart rate rising. *What in the world?* I texted back right away: "Absolutely. Let's lock it in!"

His reply took it over the top: "That's amazing, Carlos! Would [insert dollar amount here] be ok to compensate you for speaking?"

I know you won't believe me, but I'm not making this up for the sake of the story. The amount he suggested was literally within one hundred dollars of the amount I had lost from the canceled tour. THE ENTIRE TOUR. And instead of being away from my family for three weeks, I could take them with me and make it up in a single weekend. God just dropped the mic.

Everyone in the house was asleep. I slid out of bed, tiptoed down the hall, crept into the basement, and basically went loco. I was sprinting in circles yelling as loud as I could, "God, You did it! You did it! Wow, GOD, You DID IT!" I even remember doing a somersault.

Mind. Blown. I hadn't had a single booking request for weeks. WEEKS. And they were all for at least nine months out. This was crazy!

Five minutes of sprinting and I was out of breath. But I couldn't contain my excitement. I had to tell someone. So I sprinted upstairs and ran into Losiah's room. He was dead asleep. Who cares? This was his doing. He had to know. So I bent down and kissed his forehead a few times. "Buddy. Buddy, it's Daddy. Wake up." He slowly gained consciousness.

"Yeah, Dad?"

"Buddy! Remember our prayer time this afternoon? Well, guess what? I just got a text message asking me to speak at an event and guess what? It's for *exactly* the same amount I lost! Buddy! HE DID IT! GOD DID IT!" I was talking a mile a minute.

Losiah seriously, seriously replied, "Why are you so surprised, Dad? I knew He would do it. Can I go back to sleep now?"

What in the world? My son was not impressed. He simply assumed if we asked God for something, He would answer. Why wouldn't He? Man. I was undone. Never had I seen God come through so specifically in the midst of a financial battle. But I had also never used the weapon of His Word so intentionally in a financial hardship.

Friends, God's Word is real. It's available. It's living and active.

Examine your language. Pay attention to what you are speaking over your life. How often are you praying the problem instead of the promise? Everything can begin to shift today. WILD is waiting.

Oh, and one more thing. The next morning I woke up . . . to another text from another friend asking if I was available *the next weekend*. It was as if God wanted to drive this message home in a way I would never forget. I was blown away, more in awe than I had been in years.

Now I was sobbing. Heather was still sleeping.

From the time Heather fell asleep to the time she woke up, God had DOUBLED the amount of money I lost.

Only God. Only God.

REFLECT AND PRACTICE

1. When was the last time you saw God fulfill a promise in your life? I'm sad to say I don't know — He has definately fulfilled them. but my is so small I don't always recognize His promises

2. What promise is hard for you to pray right now because it is too hard to believe?

    That I will find love again; a place in His kingdom on Earth — I pray but I don't believe

3. Consider the lie—the reason the promise is too hard to believe—in your previous answer. Find a scripture that replaces the lie and write it here.

    The lies: I don't deserve it
                    I am not worthy
                    I am not loveable

    He loved me first — before I even knew him.

9

All Is Lost . . . Again

Finally, be strong in the Lord and in his mighty power. Put on the full armor of God, so that you can take your stand against the devil's schemes.

EPHESIANS 6:10–11

If you begin to forget that you are fighting a war, you will get taken out. I did. Not long after I got my swagger back, I almost lost it all again. The more I leaned into this new way of talking and walking with God, the more I felt His presence daily. The better life got, the more confidence I felt. And the more confidence I felt, the more I lost sight of the fact that it was God who was giving it to me and not me giving it to me. The healthier I got, the easier it was for me to take credit for that health. I slowly began to take my gaze off God and put it back on life.

It's so easy to do, right? None of us do it on purpose. But we definitely begin to rewrite James 1:17 as if it says, "Every good and perfect gift comes from *our hustle*." That's not what it says though. It actually says, "Every good and perfect gift is from *above*" (emphasis added). But oh how easy it is for us to lose focus and gaze at life.

It had been about a year since I returned home from Onsite, the intensive therapy program that was a big part of my journey in *Kill the Spider*. I was now applying to my life the tools for healthy living that I learned during therapy, and I was spending time hearing from God every day. It was a spiritually rich time, and my anxiety was at an all-time low. I was in a good season of life. Then, out of the blue, the season shifted in what seemed like a moment.

I remember going outside to walk our dog, Pope. We were halfway around the block when I felt a flutter in my chest. I grabbed my chest with my hand to try to feel my heart. Nothing. But then I felt another one, and the flutter seemed to happen every few seconds. *Weird,* I thought and immediately turned around to go home. When I got home, I downed a glass of water. But I kept feeling the heart flutters. What in the world? Before I knew it, I was on the one website that someone who struggles with health anxiety should never go on. Let's say it together: WebMD. Within minutes, I could feel my blood pressure rising as I started freaking myself out. I walked past Heather, and she could see the worry on my face.

"What's wrong, babe?" she asked.

"Nothing. I'm fine." And I walked into the living room and proceeded to spend two hours on my phone researching what this could be.

Hours turned into days. Days turned into weeks. Weeks turned into months. I went to the doctor but there was nothing obviously wrong. *Why was my heart doing this?* Of course, the more stressed I got, the worse the heart palpitations got too. I soon found myself in a vicious cycle of mental anxiety feeding my physical anxiety, which was feeding my mental anxiety, and so on. All the while, I *knew* I needed to be in the Word of God, yet I was spending all my time on WebMD and online forums. I was determined to defeat this thing, whatever it was. I was consumed by worry and exhausted by the mental gymnastics. I kept wondering whether everyone around me could tell that I was suffering? Friends, it got bad quickly. My anxiety came at me hard and with a vengeance. And what made me the most mad . . . was that I THOUGHT I WAS HEALED! I had told people from multiple stages that God healed my anxiety. If He had, then what was this?

Once again, I had fallen into the trap of thinking that this life was meant to be a vacation, and that all suffering would end once I began hearing from God. Day after day, I begged God for relief from the heart palpitations. Day after day, they continued. I could feel my faith slipping away. I, in turn, began to turn back to something that gave me a little bit of relief. At least I knew when I called it would answer. God wasn't answering, and suddenly my desires for an escape were too strong to resist. I won't forget the day I put those old chains back on.

I was in Montana on a work trip. My heart was fluttering really badly on this particular day. Because of that, my anxiety was through the roof as well. I remember arguing aloud with myself about the temptation I felt to start self-medicating again.

I wonder if that would bring me some relief. It worked before.

I know I promised never to do this again, but nothing else is working.

No, don't do it, Carlos. You have been free for too long. Don't.

But I wasn't strong enough to talk myself out of it. Then it happened. I put my chains back on. It had been years. And the relief lasted only a few hours. God was so kind to me. Although I chose to walk down a path of self-destruction again, my gracious God didn't let my sin go undiscovered for years as it had before. This time I got caught within days.

Three days later, I was sitting in the basement editing a video when Heather walked downstairs.

She said, "Hey. Hey, look at me. You have one shot to fix this. And I'm not talking about more therapy. We won't do this again. I need you to fix it or we are done. All the way this time, not halfway. You aren't strong enough to use just self-help tools. You need to go even deeper. Fix it. Or I'm done."

She had found out so fast. I was half relieved and half terrified. No, I hadn't gutted my family as I had a few years prior. Yet. But I was on my way. I just wanted relief. I. Wanted. To. Not. Suffer. Anymore.

Have you ever gotten to this point? The point when you're suffering so much you would risk it all for some relief? It never works out. Our attempts to solve our own problems never provide the relief we want. Chains will never bring us freedom. But I was distraught. WHY WAS GOD TAKING SO LONG TO HEAL ME?

We had to go to the mall, so Heather turned up the volume on whatever musical soundtrack the kids were listening to and adjusted the sound to the back of the minivan. I had betrayed Heather's trust again, and she wasn't going to let this spiral out of control. She said, "You have one week. I need to see evidence of progress within a week."

My heart dropped. I didn't know if I could do this. I was miserable in my own skin, and now I was miserable in my own home. I knew I had hurt Heather again and was so close to losing everything I had worked so hard to put back together.

Although my medicating behavior or "cobweb" may have been the same, the agreement with a lie or "spider" was different. Isn't that just like the Enemy? In *Kill the Spider*, I talked about how I finally killed my spider and how I broke the agreement with the lie that was causing my medicating behaviors. But the truth is, WE DON'T JUST HAVE ONE SPIDER IN OUR LIVES. We have to constantly be on the lookout for agreements we have made with lies. Suddenly, I realized I had made an agreement with another lie, which said "I will always suffer." Although I didn't know it at the time, the wrong belief that my suffering would never end was what was taking me down this black hole of despair. And my solution was to do anything possible to find relief.

A Last-Ditch Effort

By this point in our journey, I had done *so much* work. I had been through so much therapy. But there was a strategy I hadn't yet tried. People have different names for it. Some people call it Inner Healing, while others call it Sozo or Freedom Prayer. No matter what you call it, it involves somebody facilitating Holy Spirit–led prayer for healing from whatever bondage you have been in, which leads you to freedom. It's basically a Kill the Spider session on steroids. And because I already knew what went on in those sessions, I was wary of trying Freedom Prayer. I knew how to identify the lie, corner it, and kill it. I knew all that.

Although I hadn't yet written *Kill the Spider*, I had already implemented the process of identifying lies and breaking agreements that I outlined in the book. While that process was an important foundation and essential for finding freedom, I hadn't yet experienced the depth and intensity of a Freedom Prayer session, which is more like Navy Seal training in spiritual warfare. Many books have been written and still could be written on spiritual warfare, so this section is in no way meant to be an exhaustive thesis on the topic. But my hope is that it will be enough to get you to the place where you can approach spiritual battles with confidence, maybe even some swagger. Remember, the only tactic the Enemy has in this war is getting you to believe his lies. Throw truth at him, and he doesn't know what to do.

Because I was fighting another round in my fight for freedom, I needed more than just basic training. The Enemy was on to me, and he was suddenly using more advanced techniques in his attacks. In this season, I needed special ops. I needed spiritual help from someone who knew how to fight using warfare prayer. This time around, it would require targeting these lies specifically and with accuracy.

I talked with some close friends and learned about a man named John who had the experience I was looking for. I googled him and found his website. Nope. It looked like it had been built in 1998 on a Yahoo! GeoCities page. The background color was turquoise, and there was an animated GIF of a glowing cross at the top center. The font looked like Comic Sans, and there was no way this dude was going to be able to help

me. But my back was up against the wall. Heather had given me a week to
make some progress. So I emailed him.

> Good evening, John. My name is Carlos Whittaker and I am on
> the brink of losing everything I love because I can't seem to stop
> my anxiety and all that it brings. Nothing is working and my
> self-medicating is hurting those I love the most. I'd love to meet
> if you have an appointment free. Thanks.

Perfect, I thought. *I sent him an email. That should be enough to meet
Heather's demands.* Obviously, I would start looking for someone else next
week—someone whose website was up to date. Three minutes later, I received a phone call from a Nashville-area number that wasn't in my phone.
I let it go to voice mail. When I listened to it, I heard this: "Hello, Carlos?
This is John. I'm just calling you after I received your email. Listen, I'm
extremely booked up but would love to talk to you for a few minutes to see
if I can point you in the right direction. Give me a call when you get this."

Great! I thought. *Old-school dude doesn't have time. Maybe he can
recommend someone a bit more me.* I called him back. Friends, within
sixty seconds of being on the phone with John, I was in tears. I can't quite
remember what he said or how he said it, but I do remember it felt as if I
was talking to someone who spent all day every day talking to God. Suddenly, I was less concerned with checking something off my list; instead, I
was seeing an opportunity to rid myself of this anxiety once and for all. I
found myself begging to meet with him.

"John, I know you said you are booked up, but I'll pay double. I'll pay
triple. I need your help, man. What can I do?"

John heard the desperation in my voice. "Carlos, what about tomorrow morning at seven o'clock? Can you meet me then? We will have to be
done by nine o'clock in time for my first appointment, but I'll make time
for you tomorrow."

The next day at 6:55 a.m., I was parked in his driveway. But this wasn't just any driveway. Imagine the driveway of Highclere Castle, the setting for *Downton Abbey*. It was just like that and led to a house that looked like a smaller replica of Highclere Castle. If you aren't a fan of PBS historical dramas, then just imagine the mansion you want in heaven. Like this place was *baller*.

"I thought this dude was a hokey old prayer minister?" I mumbled to myself. What in the world did he do? Maybe this wasn't his house. Maybe he gave me the wrong address. I got out, walked to the front, and knocked on the door. I was half expecting a butler to answer it. From somewhere inside I heard, "Carlos! Can you meet me at the library door? I'm so sorry! Just walk about fifty yards to the left!"

The library door? He has a library? That has its own entrance? I walked down a sidewalk in the front of his home around the side to another wing. This must be the library. He was already there waiting for me at the door. He had a smile that could win any presidential election, piercing blue eyes, and white hair slicked back to reveal a weathered but handsome face. *This is the dude,* I thought, *who is gonna lead me to freedom.*

"Come in, Carlos. Can I get you some tea?" he asked.

"Sure, man. Thanks," I replied.

He headed to the kitchen to grab the tea.

The library was large, about a thousand square feet. Floor-to-ceiling shelves filled with books lined the room. The ceilings had to be at least twenty feet high, and there was a rolling ladder on each wall so one could get to said books. There was also an indoor balcony wrapping around half of the room. Everything was solid oak. And there were massive windows, one on the east side of the room and one on the west. In the middle of the room sat two chairs facing each other. A small table stood next to each of the chairs; one had a glass of water and notepad while a box of tissues rested on the other. A small trash bin stood nearby. I quickly made the correct assumption that John would be sitting in the chair with the notepad taking notes and sipping his water, while I would be in the other chair wiping off the tears and snot and then disposing of said tissue in the small trash bin.

"Sit. Sit, Carlos," John said, surprising me as he walked back in.

I sat down as he handed me my tea.

Then he sat down in his chair. He was about two feet away from me. He locked eyes with me without saying anything at all. I felt *extremely* uncomfortable yet also completely comfortable. I had never met this man, but I felt as if he knew every single thing about me.

He just smiled and stared at me. I stared back. Are you picking up on the weirdness yet? I need you to, because it was weird. Finally, after a few minutes of awkward silence for me, he asked, "Why are you here, Carlos?"

That was the million-dollar question. Why was I there? I thought I was there so he could help me stop the heart palpitations and anxiety, so I could get some relief. But what I didn't know was that God wasn't going to let me go back to relief. He wasn't going to let me get halfway to abundance again.

No, this time relief would be replaced by revival.

BUT NOT WITHOUT A FIGHT. Not without a war.

REFLECT AND PRACTICE

1. What are the medicating behaviors you are constantly trying and failing to get rid of? Write them down.

   Overeating
   Watching too much TV
   Playing games (Procrastination)

2. List the specific tactics you have used to try to get rid of them.

   Diets, diets, diets.
   Deleting games & recordings
   Hiding Ipad   Self-condemnation
   Prayer
   Journalling

10

This Is How We Fight

Our struggle is not against flesh and blood, but against the rulers, against the authorities, against the powers of this dark world and against the spiritual forces of evil in the heavenly realms. Therefore put on the full armor of God, so that when the day of evil comes, you may be able to stand your ground, and after you have done everything, to stand.

EPHESIANS 6:12–13

Right now, every single person reading this is in the war. Notice I said *the* war. Because although each of us may be fighting different battles, it is all the same war. This war is not being waged between flesh and blood in the natural world. Certain battles may take place here on earth and involve our physical and material lives, but it is in the supernatural realm that the ultimate war is happening. As you read just above, "Our struggle is not against flesh and blood, but against the rulers, against the authorities, against the powers of this dark world and against the spiritual forces of evil in the heavenly realms."

What I find fascinating is that even if someone doesn't believe that there is a spiritual war going on, that person is not exempt from being a participant in said war. Even those who deny the existence of God and claim Christianity is a lie are engaged in this war. It is happening with or without our acknowledgment.

The same principle applies to our readiness for this war. Some of us might believe there is a war, but all we are carrying into battle is a Nerf gun and some foam darts. Still others may be training for this war daily and have special-ops-like skills. But no matter your skill set, you are *in the war*. Together. Fighting alongside one another. Again, we are all in the same war, just fighting different battles. Those of you struggling with anxiety and depression are standing alongside others struggling with cancer and heart conditions. Same war. Different battles. You may be fighting pornography, but you are fighting alongside someone fighting gossip. Perhaps you're battling workaholism beside a neighbor who is fighting alcoholism. Same war, different battles.

Weapons of Our Warfare

However, the good news is that we do have effective tools and tactics to use as we engage in this spiritual war. These tools will equip you to fight all the battles you face, while making significant progress for the forces of good in the spiritual realm. No matter your specific struggle, these strategies will work for you. By using these tactics, you can experience peace and victory.

- Speaking the Word of God
- Worshipping God
- Overcoming the Enemy's lies
- Intercessory prayer

We talked about speaking the Word of God over our lives in a previous chapter, but another of the best ways to use the truth of God's Word is to sing it. What some would call worship music is a powerful way to sing

God's truths over our lives. This is why we feel so empowered after singing praise and worship songs, especially when they are based on Scripture (which I hope they are!). When we sing these songs, we are singing biblical truths over our lives!

The worship song "Raise a Hallelujah" by Bethel Music is a perfect example of this:

> I raise a hallelujah, in the presence of my enemies . . .
> I raise a hallelujah, my weapon is a melody[10]

Do you see? What does a worship song melody consist of? Well, hopefully it is based on scriptural truths. This song is particularly powerful since the core message is based on the word *hallelujah,* which literally means "God be praised." Another song called "Surrounded (Fight My Battles)" by UPPERROOM says:

> So my weapons are praise and thanksgiving
> This is how I fight my battles[11]

In this song, the line "This is how I fight my battles" expresses the power of lifting a song of praise for what God has done. When we take the Word of God and wrap it in a melody, we are able to declare these God-breathed truths over our lives. This is why worship is so powerful. It's not the moving lights and smoky haze, the amazingly creative music videos on YouTube, or the incredibly influential churches that create these songs. No, the reason worship is so powerful is because WE ARE LITERALLY DECLARING THE TRUTHS OF GOD'S WORD OVER OUR LIVES. We are engaging in warfare every time we sing these songs, whether we're in a corporate worship setting or sitting in our living rooms. This is warfare. It's not a time to sit with a latte in your right hand and your phone in your left.

This is how we fight our battles! And as we mature, our technique also matures. I spent the majority of my Christian life praying and asking God to take away certain situations. I would pray that God would remove circumstances from my life. For instance, I asked God to take away my anxiety, to encourage me, or to make me stronger. Although these sorts of prayers are fine, sometimes they are dodging the issue at hand. We read in James 4:7, "Submit yourselves, then, to God. Resist the devil, and he will flee from you."

Too many Christians are living as if that verse says, "Ignore the devil, and he will flee from you." That's how many of us have translated this verse. But, friends! That's not what it says! The Greek word *anthistēmi*, which is translated in this verse as *resist*, means "to set one's self against, to withstand, resist, oppose."[12] Resisting doesn't sound as simple as praying a passive prayer, does it? No. This verse makes it sound as if we're setting up for the crane kick at the end of *The Karate Kid* that put Johnny Lawrence flat on his back (by the way, that may be one of the best scenes in eighties movie history). Let's keep going with this illustration. Daniel didn't pray that God would take that bully Johnny away. Instead, he got into the fighting position he had been trained to assume when his back was against the wall, and he delivered the blow to the enemy.

We need to be like Daniel-san. We already have the skills and bravery to RESIST THE ENEMY instead of just ignoring him. Instead of the crane kick, we have prayer and the Word of God, which are much more effective tactics.

Now let's pause for a second because I know there are some people reading this book who, when they hear anything about spiritual warfare or the Holy Spirit, are basically like "I'm out." And I get it. Because these both have been abused for far too long in the church. The Holy Spirit has been used as a tool to manipulate people out of money, while the term *spiritual warfare* has been used to manipulate people and their emotions. Not more than five years ago, I was right there with you guys. I wasn't about to let anyone emotionally manipulate me. And I was SO GUARDED. Why? Because I wanted to stay safe. That makes sense. But, friends, these weapons we have at our disposal are so effective.

Another tool I use in this spiritual war is the following prayer exercise, which removes any power the Enemy has over certain situations in my life. There are four key words or steps in this process: confess, renounce, reject, and replace. Once God has revealed to me any lie I have been operating under (and He reveals these to us once we Enter Rest), I pray through these four words or actions.

Confess (1 John 1:9)

When we realize we have been believing something counter to God's promises, the first thing we need to do is confess that we have believed a lie and lost our belief in the truth. Whether the promises are about who we are or God's character or plans for us, we must come clean and ask forgiveness for our unbelief in His truth. Regardless of the specific lie, it's critical to start here.

Renounce (Titus 2:11–15)

Once we have asked for God's forgiveness, we have to take it a step further and renounce the lie. This means we refuse to live our lives according to that lie any longer. Although Jesus can hear us no matter how we pray, I love to pray confidently aloud that I will no longer act in accordance with Satan's lies. This step helps us leave behind the lie that has been keeping us bound for so long.

Reject (Acts 16:16–18)

This is the point in the prayer where we have to get specific. By using Scripture to outline the particular ways we will reject the lie and step into the truth, we will reject every lie that Jesus has revealed to us.

Replace (James 4:7)

Whenever we eliminate something from our lives, a void or gap will be revealed. That is why we must quickly refill the space in our spirit vacated by this lie. If we don't, the Enemy will try to fill it with another lie or error. Wrap up your prayer by asking Jesus to come heal and restore this space.[13]

If you implement these strategies for spiritual warfare—speaking the truth of God's Word over your life, praising and worshipping God, claiming victory over the Enemy's lies, and practicing intercessory prayer—you will be able to move from level one to level ten. You will go from white belt to ninja. I promise. Try it. You will see changes immediately.

Back to the library . . .

REFLECT AND PRACTICE

Look back at the questions at the end of the previous chapter and the behaviors you keep trying to fix. Ask God to *specifically* reveal to you the lies you believe that are in turn producing these behaviors. (These don't have to be deep or lifelong behaviors.)

> Dear Lord, Please reveal to me the lies I believe that continue to produce over-indulgent, procrastinating behaviors in my life. In Jesus name,
> Amen

11

All the Parts of Me

The dominant characteristic of an authentic spiritual
life is the gratitude that flows from trust—not only for
all the gifts that I receive from God, but gratitude for
all the suffering. Because in that purifying experience suffering has often been the shortest path to
intimacy with God.

BRENNAN MANNING

"Why am I here?" I repeated the question John had asked me.

"Yes, that's what I asked. Tell me, Carlos, why are you here?" he
reiterated.

"John, I want relief. I'm so exhausted from all this anxiety. It's crushing me. I feel like I can't breathe. And I know all the verses that tell me to
trust God and not to worry and stuff, but it's not working. So I was hoping
I could come here and you could pray for me. Maybe cast something out
of me or something? I don't know. But what I do know is that this is my
last shot." I was crying by this point. Even though I was all in, I was still a
bit jaded and distrusting of this entire process. "So do you want me to

stand up or something? Put my hands out with my palms up? Tell me how this works. I'm ready," I continued.

John smiled the kind of smile you give your kid when she tells you about her imaginary friend. You don't want to burst her bubble, but you also want to make sure she doesn't keep Squiggles the Pink Elephant around until she's twenty-five. "Oh, Carlos. This isn't going to be some magic show. And actually, I'm not going to do anything. You are in charge of your own FREEDOM. I'm just along for the ride."

Along for the ride? I'm paying him money just to come along for the ride?

"I'm just here to help you hear. Maybe help you see. But I'm not going to be casting anything out of you. I'm not going to be yelling. If there is any emotion, it will come from you, Carlos, not me."

Well, I had some bad news for John. I had been trying to get rid of this worry and anxiety by myself for years. Decades even. I felt defeated before we even started.

"You can do this, Carlos. You are not the exception to the promises of Scripture. All the healing you read about—that's for you. And today it will happen."

That was a mighty brave thing of him to say. But once again, I found myself with no other options. *So let's give this thing a go, why don't we.*

John asked again why I was there, and I went into more detail than you want to know about my initial medicating behavior that led to the implosion of my marriage and life as I knew it. I told him about going to Onsite and how impactful that had been for me. I detailed the strides I had made in my healing and how I promised myself I'd never let those impulses control me again. I told him about the agreements I had made with lies and how I had identified and destroyed them. Or thought I had. I told him how confusing and disappointing it was to slip up again since I thought I killed that part of me. I told him how Heather had given me an ultimatum and how terrified I was that I didn't have the strength to overcome because the old me seemed stronger than the new me.

John was scribbling furiously as I spoke. Every so often, he looked up at me and paused, then went back to scribbling again. I didn't realize it, but his pauses occurred every single time I talked about the "old me" or the other "part of me." When I finally finished catching him up on my story, which probably took forty-five minutes or so, he looked up at me and smiled. *Why did he keep smiling?*

He began to speak, "Carlos, I think I know where we need to start. And to be honest, it may be where we need to end as well. Did you know God designed our brains in such a way that we are able to walk through trauma and still function day to day? Life is impossibly hard. But we as humans have a place for the pain to go, and we don't have to feel it. Because our brain, in God's glorious design, takes that pain and tucks it away. So, fear is not a bad thing. It keeps us alert so that we don't feel pain. Anger and addictions are doing much the same thing. They are protecting us from pain. Just so you know, the anxiety and worry that you want to get rid of—God created those things in our limbic system so that you are protected from pain."

This was fascinating stuff. But I had a problem. It seriously sounded like he was saying MY ANXIETY WAS GOOD.

"So what we are going to do here is called heart sync. We are going to attempt to connect the part of your heart that walked in here with the part of your heart that is gripped in fear 24/7 and the part of your heart that keeps making bad medicating decisions."

"Wait a second," I jumped in. "Why would I want to connect back to the fearful part of me? Don't we want to get rid of it?" I finished.

"Ahh, now you are beginning to understand and connect that there are various parts of your heart. We don't want to get rid of that part of you, Carlos. That is a part of you that God made. We want to reconnect and bring healing to that part of you."

John continued. "All this isn't as crazy as it sounds. It's biblical. Let's look at the king of emotions: David. He was doing the work we will be doing in here all the time. When he wrote, 'Why, my soul, are you down-cast? . . . Put your hope in God' in Psalm 42, he was essentially talking to the downcast part of his soul. He was in communion with that part of him. And if there is anyone in Scripture who can make us feel less bipolar than we are, it's David. He goes from Psalm 143 where he is crying and begging God for mercy because he feels as if God is crushing his soul to Psalm 145 where he is praising God's greatness. But he is talking to all parts of his heart and listening to his heart nonstop. He is connected to his heart. It is synced. The 'good' parts and the 'bad' parts. Do you see how different David's relationship with his heart is from yours?"

Silence. I was waiting for him to continue.

"That's not a rhetorical question, Carlos. What's different about how David relates to all parts of his soul compared with how you and most of humanity do it?"

More silence.

Then like a slap in the face, it hit me. It's why he kept pausing when I was initially spilling my guts to him. I'm the opposite of David. (Which isn't all bad, TBH.) But there is a part of David that I do want to emulate, and I was failing at that. I wanted *absolutely zero* to do with the parts of me that cause pain and anxiety. I literally would ask God to intervene using words like "kill that part of me." I wanted to lock part of my soul in a cell and throw away the key. But my freedom wouldn't be found in taking captive and prosecuting those parts of me. I realized my freedom would actually be found in restoring relationship and engaging with those parts of me.

Mind. Blown.

How often do we do this? We look at parts of ourselves and, instead of entering into relationship with those parts of our hearts and finding healing, we try to suppress them, feeling angry at them and afraid of them. We end up in self-rejection, self-conflict, and self-condemnation. That in turn makes it impossible for us to actually release those parts of ourselves from the chains.

I know that is a lot to digest. It was for me. It's so contrary to what I'd been taught. And although my mind was coming alive in this teaching from John, I did have a big roadblock.

"Okay. So I need to not lock away the part of me that feels fear or even the part of me that caused so much pain for my family and friends, but what about all the scriptures telling us to get rid of things like fear, promiscuity, worry, and drunkenness? I'm not really able to resolve what you are saying with the instruction to get rid of the anxiety and medicating behavior."

"Great question, Carlos. Let me say it like this. You drove over here frustrated and angry about the you that is carrying all the fear and anxiety. But both of you are welcome here. You see, it is actually *you* feeling the fear. And it is *you* who is frustrated and wanting the fear to leave. Both parts of you are welcome here.

"I know the pain and frustration of living with feelings that will not go away, feelings that you would very much like to go away. The heart palpitations. The dizziness. The physical symptoms of anxiety. The worry. The panic. I know how overwhelming it is to live with these things and not feel any reprieve from their assault. And you read Scripture and feel horrible because it is telling you that you should not be feeling all these things, that you should be feeling and experiencing shalom, but you are not. That can be so frustrating. But I want you to consider that you are feeling that fear for a very good reason. And although I understand wanting to stand against that fear, I need the part of you that is carrying that fear to know you are welcome here. Again, you are welcome here and the fear you carry is welcome here."

Now he was talking to me as if I had multiple personalities, talking to different parts of me, but I was beginning to understand where he was going.

"I need you to know I understand demonic oppression. I understand evil. I've worked in various deliverance ministries for more than thirty

years. And you, my friend, both the part of you that is carrying this fear
and the part of you that made decisions that destroyed your family—both
of those parts of you are not evil. And they are welcome here. The goal here
is not to get loud and cast fear out of the room. The goal is for you to come
back into relationship with those parts of you that are using fear and addictions to keep you safe. Once you are back in relationship with those
parts of you, good relationship, then we invite Jesus to be in relationship
with those parts of you that have yet to experience the peace He brings.
You see, it is Jesus, His perfect love, that casts out fear. Not our emotion.
But Jesus and His love."

It was all beginning to click. And I hope it is with you guys too. Those
parts of you that you have been hating all these years? I was about to see
firsthand that it's our own self-hate, our own self-judgment, that keeps
those parts of us bound to what only His perfect love can cast out.

It's like that teddy bear you had as a child. In my case, it was a stuffed
Kermit the Frog. I had an eighties version with Velcro on his hands and
feet so I could attach him anywhere. I could not fall asleep without Kermit. He made me feel so safe. But the truth was that there was actually
nothing special about Kermit. In all actuality, homeboy's hands and feet
scratched my face up every night. So if it wasn't Kermit keeping me safe,
what was it? It was the *idea* of Kermit keeping me safe. The stuffed frog
had no power, but I gave it power.

"Carlos, I want you to come back very soon. I think we are close. But
I have another appointment and our two hours have come to an end. Next
time, you are going to walk out of here and your heart palpitations will not
follow you. I believe this with all my heart. Do you?" John asked.

I nodded yes. And I was waiting for my heart to shake no. But it
didn't. It was suddenly aligned with my head. What was happening? Did
I *really* believe John could pray some magic prayer over me to make these
anxiety symptoms disappear? No. Actually I didn't. But you know who I
did believe could pray and make them go away? Me.

I stood up, hugged John (I don't think I was supposed to do that because it turned into an awkward side hug), and walked out the door.

I left there with my two new friends: anxious, fearful me and artificial-intimacy-medicating me. The three of us were about to have a moment that I will never forget.

REFLECT AND PRACTICE

Ask God to reveal to you how you may have been judging or hating certain parts of yourself. Write these down, reflecting on how this has affected you. What have you lost by judging, hating, or ignoring something God wants to heal and redeem?

12

Beet Juice

Give thanks to the LORD, for he is good;
his love endures forever.

1 Chronicles 16:34

Let's pause for a second and speak to the elephant in the room. Carlos the Baptist was asking for help from Inner Healing Charismatic John. I've got most of you on board by this point, and I'm fairly certain I'll have the rest of you by the end of the book. But some of you have been so wounded by the charismatic culture, and the trust may be too broken to rebuild in a hundred pages. You may actually want no part of WILD. You've seen enough that I can totally understand why you'd want to settle for MILD.

Stay with me. Every day after I work out, I stop by a juice bar off Franklin Road in Brentwood, Tennessee. I stop in every day to drink beet juice. You read that right: beet juice. If you know me personally, you know that when I get into something, I get into it. Can I list for you some of the health benefits of beet juice? DON'T SKIP THIS PART! You'll be ordering beets and a juicer before you get to the end of the paragraph.

Beet juice increases blood flow. It lowers blood pressure. It increases energy and stamina. It removes toxins from the liver. It reduces the risks of getting cancer. It helps protect against anemia and iron deficiency. It gives you healthy, glowing skin. And it helps prevent constipation.[14]

Now that the senior-citizen ad is over and it's extremely clear that I'm a middle-aged man in his forties, go ahead and place that label over my life. These days I'm much more interested in what goes on inside my body than how I look with my shirt off. Although, yes, I still flex in the mirror when I'm shirtless. Will that ever stop? I hope not. Back to the beets.

So what does beet juice have to do with conversational intimacy with Jesus? What does a beet have to do with us finally Entering Wild? Let's begin with the beet itself. Hang in there, meat-and-potato-loving friends. I promise this little aside will be worth it.

Look at all those benefits that drinking beet juice achieves. I mean seriously! Why do we even attempt eating anything else? It's basically a superfood. It does everything but attempt an actual burpee for you. When you drink it, it's as if your insides are doing burpees all day and night and getting in the best shape of their lives. It's incredibly healthy. There is nothing unhealthy about it. The benefits far outweigh any struggle to come to grips with the taste.

Right. The taste. I know that is where I lost some of you guys. I mean, have you ever had a beet that your grandma steamed and then sprinkled with a little salt and pepper? Cleanup on aisle beet. Those things made me want to vomit the second I put them in my piehole. I used to *hate* the taste of beets. I couldn't stomach them. I had tasted them before, and they were really, really bad.

In a similar way, many of you have been avoiding the Holy Spirit altogether because you kinda get the same thing happening in your stomach. You've tasted a version of Him that you can't stomach. So much gross. You think, *Been there, done that. Not gonna try that again.* That's fair. But you also know all the benefits that come with Holy Spirit, right? You've read the scriptures. You have heard the sermons. You know He is vital to your well-being. But you just can't stomach Him the way you have tried Him before.

GOOD NEWS! You don't have to.

You see, there is nothing worse than having a good thing that has been cooked incorrectly. It doesn't have to be beets. It can be anything. The food may be healthy, but if it's not prepared right, it's likely to taste awful.

Now, before the theology police come after me, I'm not saying we actually have to cook the Holy Spirit. We don't have to season the Holy Spirit either. But you do see where I'm going. We have all seen religion completely destroy the credibility of Jesus. I've seen pastors use Jesus as a prop for their political aspirations. I've seen pastors use the Holy Spirit as a manipulation tool to increase tithes and offerings. But just because their humanity got in the way of showing us the divinity of the Trinity, DOESN'T MAKE THE TRINITY ANY LESS DIVINE. And we can even give these humans the benefit of the doubt. We all have messed up a really good thing before. Just because my grandma steamed and salted those nasty beets, she didn't make the beets any less healthy.

So what if I told you that entering into true communion with Holy Spirit would blow away any "cooked up" experience you have ever had with Him? What if I told you that it's not gonna be weird, that it's not going to taste disgusting?

Psalm 34:8 tells us, "Taste and see that the LORD is good." I don't think it was an accident that David used two of our senses to explain how we can experience the goodness of God.

We get to experience the power of the Holy Spirit with all our senses. And I think that if you stay with me for a few more chapters, you won't want MILD anymore. Kinda like me after I left John's house the second time. I was ready to see something WILD.

The Missing Piece

When I got home after that first visit, I sprinted into my office. Contrary to this label, the space in question was the basement sofa with a half-folded laundry pile on it. I immediately grabbed my headphones, put them in my ears, and hit Play on the recording of the session I had just finished (recorded with John's permission). I fast-forwarded to the part where John said we were going to reconnect the different parts of myself. The prospect of this still scared me. But if John said it was going to work, then I was game. However, while I was literally in the middle of listening to the recording, my heart started fluttering and doing that palpitation thing again.

"Ugh. I'm so tired of . . . !" I began to exclaim aloud, but then I stopped before I could finish. I realized something. I had not had a heart palpitation since I went in to see John. SERIOUSLY. Those PVCs, as my doctor called them, were harmless. Yet they completely sucked the life out of a worrier like me. Every day when I woke up in the morning, the first thought that ran through my head was, *When is it gonna happen?* And normally before I even got up, my heart began doing PVCs. Basically I was waiting for the pain to hit instead of just enjoying the respite. Oh, the endless cycle of anxiety.

But this was the first time in over three hours that my heart had fluttered. Friends, it had been weeks of nonstop PVCs, with never more than a ten-minute break. And John hadn't prayed for them to go away. Why did they go away for a few hours? Why were they back? Did I think something wrong while on the sofa? Did I get stressed about something? Next thing I knew I was back on Google, searching for reasons they were happening. One thing led me to another, which led me to a forum including someone who had been suffering from these things every ten minutes for thirty years. My mind began to race. *Maybe that's my destiny as well? Maybe . . .*

"Carlos? Are you down there? Why are you in the basement? I wanna hear about your prayer appointment. Are you free to talk?"

Ugh. It was just like Heather to interrupt a perfectly fine session of Google despair.

As I walked upstairs, I was more keenly aware of the distinct parts of my heart. One part of me was focused on healing, while another part focused on the worry and pain. When I rounded the corner and saw Heather standing in the kitchen, I considered the other part of me that John and I had just talked about that ruined everything by medicating my anxiety. The part of me that had lost all Heather's trust in 2010. That part of me was right there as well.

"So tell me. How was it?" Heather asked.

"Can I ask you something first, babe?" I interrupted her quest for information. "I need to know something. How did you forgive the part of me that medicated with artificial intimacy, that made those choices and destroyed all the trust that you had in me? How did you forgive that part of me?" I could tell she was a bit perplexed. She hadn't just spent two hours with a handsome Holy Spirit whisperer in his multimillion-dollar library learning the ins and outs of how God designed our brains to protect us from trauma.

"I don't really know the full workings of how that all happened, but I do know this. Everybody wanted us to get a divorce. And I was fine with that. But the closer I got to Jesus, the more I stopped looking at the medicating behavior that ended it all. I kept seeing you as if you'd been in a car wreck. There was all this internal bleeding, this massive trauma. Yet all anyone wanted to do was focus on a broken finger, as if that was what ended it. But the broken finger wasn't the problem. There were bigger problems. By looking at the bigger picture, I was able to forgive you for the broken finger a lot more easily. Forgiveness was the beginning for me. I still didn't think reconciliation was going to happen, but forgiving you was a way that I could find freedom. But once the forgiveness took root in me, and God started doing a new work in you, reconciliation could happen. But not without forgiveness. That was the key."

I don't really know if Heather answered my question, but I do know that she answered *a question,* which was how did she find it in her to let me back in? Was she looking at the bigger picture again? Although the gravity of my latest offense wasn't nearly as monumental as the previous (trust me, I mean that in the eyes of the world and not in the eyes of my marriage), she obviously was still looking at the overall trauma as opposed to the broken finger.

She continued. "That doesn't mean that this won't end. That doesn't mean I'm going through that again. But I've seen the work you're doing and that God is doing in you, and it's just not done yet."

Forgiveness. Forgiveness unlocked the potential in our marriage. Forgiveness unlocked the freedom and impossible peace I talked about in the beginning of the book. Was it forgiveness that I needed now? But I was the one who did all this, the one who kept screwing up. Whom was I supposed to forgive? Maybe the other person in that artificial relationship that had taken down my marriage. Yep. I bet that's the ticket. Or maybe my old boss who told me I just needed to have more faith in order to get rid of my anxiety. Yeah. Okay. I had a list of people I was ready to forgive when I walked back into John's library. *Look at this prepared healthy version of me ready for all the healing!*

A few days later, on Friday at seven o'clock, I pulled up in front of John's house. Walked in. Sat down. Smiled at John. Caught him up on my convo with Heather. Told him I was ready. He seemed a bit unnerved by my eagerness.

"Okay, Carlos. Let's invite Holy Spirit to come and direct us where we need to go today. Would that be all right with you?" John asked gently.

"Oh. I already know where we need to go today, John," I said. "Last night when Heather was telling me about how forgiveness freed her, I knew what I needed to do today. So I'm ready to forgive."

John seemed delighted in my acknowledgment that forgiveness would be key. "Yes, Carlos! You got it! So are you ready? I think this is going to be powerful."

"Yeah, man. I am. Who should I start with first? My boss who made me feel like my anxiety was all in my head?"

Immediately John cocked his head to the left and smiled that same smile he had thrown at me during the first visit. "Oh, Carlos, I see where you ended up. And although forgiveness is going to be the key to you finding freedom, it's not going to be forgiving anyone but yourself." He said this very matter of factly.

Forgive myself?

What in the world? This wasn't what I had seen coming. But it was also the exact direction I needed to go to begin the process of being completely and totally healed of any and all anxiety. And it started with self-forgiveness.

REFLECT AND PRACTICE

1. What are some situations in your life for which you still hold judgment of yourself?

2. Consider those situations. Write down where you need to forgive yourself; in other words, what specific actions did you take in those situations that need forgiveness?

13

Roadblocks

Let all bitterness and wrath and anger and
clamor and slander be put away from you,
along with all malice. Be kind to one another,
tenderhearted, forgiving one another, as God
in Christ forgave you.

EPHESIANS 4:31–32, ESV

We all have made agreements with lies. Those agreements in turn produce behaviors we are all trying to fix. And when we discover those agreements and break them, we find freedom. It's a simple concept. Yet there is also a complicated thing that keeps many people from pulling this off: unforgiveness. Unforgiveness prevents many Christians from experiencing the WILD that God has for them. You. Yes, you reading this book, you have more abundance waiting for you on the other side of forgiveness.

When our kids were young and got into a fight, we would always make them apologize to each other and then forgive each other. To be honest, we still make them do this, and they are teenagers. I'll never forget the time I asked Seanna to ask Sohaila's forgiveness for hurting her. I can't remember the exact situation, but there was blood involved, and I could tell Seanna actually felt bad. Lots of screaming from her five-year-old sister and lots of feeling bad about it from the four-year-old.

"I'm swawwy, Sohaila. I didn't mean to hwuut you. Will you forgive me?" said Seanna.

Please tell me you read that with an adorable four-year-old lisp.

To Seanna's surprise, Sohaila said, "I forgive you," and immediately jumped up to go and play on the trampoline.

Seanna looked perplexed when her previously impaired sister was suddenly healed and able to run off to play. I'll never forget this. Ever.

Seanna ran straight up to Sohaila and said, "Never mind. I thought you were more hurt. I take back my sorry."

Isn't this the case with us too? Our forgiveness is so wrapped up in our own emotions. This is *not* the kind of forgiveness God is talking about in Scripture. The godly forgiveness we are talking about here is the PRIMARY POSTURE that will lead us all to abundance and freedom, to WILD. As long as there is any sort of unforgiveness in our hearts, our path toward life to the full will be blocked. Unforgiveness is an actual roadblock with no way around it.

We won't ever get to experience all that God has for us unless we truly understand what forgiveness is. So let's define it. I like how Chester and Betsy Kylstra define it in their book *Biblical Healing and Deliverance:* "Forgiveness is the principal activity and heart attitude needed to pave the way for freedom."[15] You see, what happens when we choose to forgive someone is that we are actually releasing *them* into freedom. Them. Not us. Do you see the massive difference? No more plans of retaliation. No more secretly resenting them from afar. No more waiting for them to offer some sort of sacrifice in return. No, they are free. The dictionary gives us this definition of *forgive:* "to cease to feel resentment against."[16] But I actually like the definition of *pardon* better, which is "the excusing of an offense without exacting a penalty."[17] This is what the gospel offers. God the Father doesn't just cease to feel resentment against us. No. He actually pardons us. That's divine forgiveness.

DIVINE FORGIVENESS? Yes, ma'am. Now we're talking.

It's clear from Scripture how essential forgiveness is for us to live life to the full. Mark 11:25 reads, "When you stand praying, if you hold anything against anyone, forgive them, so that your Father in heaven may forgive you your sins." Now I'm not going to go so far as to say that God *will not* forgive us if we are not forgiving our brothers and sisters, but I will say IT SEEMS PRETTY IMPORTANT TO GOD HERE.

Just after Jesus shares His famous method for prayer, He says, "If you forgive other people when they sin against you, your heavenly Father will also forgive you" (Matthew 6:14). There is clearly a correlation between forgiving others and receiving God's love. Again, I don't think it's because God is withholding forgiveness from us. I think we are the ones who keep His full forgiveness at arm's length when we don't actively forgive those who have sinned against us.

Once more in the gospel of Matthew, Jesus speaks to this topic with the parable of the unmerciful servant. Jesus concludes by saying, "This is how my heavenly Father will treat each of you unless you forgive your brother or sister from your heart" (18:35).

Yep. Forgiveness seems to be *essential* in our walk with God. As we saw in this last verse, it has to be gut-level forgiveness. This is not the shallow Seanna-at-four-years-old kind of forgiveness.

When we enter into that heart forgiveness, we can lean into verses such as 1 John 1:9: "If we confess our sins, he is faithful and just and will forgive us our sins and purify us from all unrighteousness." There it is. The entire gospel seems strongly linked to forgiveness. In fact, it is at the crux of our salvation and, I would add, our satisfaction in life on this side of heaven. Forgiveness unlocks it all.

Three Types of Forgiveness

When we don't forgive, healing literally cannot happen. This isn't just a biblical truth; scientific research shows that unforgiveness can prevent us from moving forward and can have a negative impact on our physical health as well.[18] Even secular psychologists agree that unforgiveness holds our brains and bodies captive, preventing us from being the healthiest we can be.[19] So when we forgive, we begin the healing process. According to Chester and Betsy Kylstra, there are three types of forgiveness that need to unfold in order for us to unlock freedom in our lives and hearts: our forgiveness of others, God's forgiveness of us, and our forgiveness of ourselves.[20]

The first type of forgiveness, then, is your forgiveness of others. You, mi amigo or mi amiga, reading this book right now, you have some forgiveness yet to give. God never asked us to forgive someone 99 percent of the way. No. He wants us to forgive them with total 100 percent forgiveness. So 99 percent does not send us into the WILD. Only full, complete forgiveness will. In the gospel of Matthew, Jesus told the disciples about the need for unlimited forgiveness: "Then Peter came to Jesus and asked, 'Lord, how many times shall I forgive my brother or sister who sins against me? Up to seven times?' Jesus answered, 'I tell you, not seven times, but seventy-seven times'" (18:21–22).

Too often people can't seem to get to the place where they *feel* like they can forgive someone, and that becomes a roadblock. Their pain seems too great, and they can't even fathom forgiving the person who caused it. GREAT NEWS! Forgiveness isn't a feeling. It is a decision. It is a decision to set someone free from the expectation of your punishment. You don't have to feel like it. Just open your hands and make a decision to forgive. Now. Since forgiveness isn't a feeling, it won't immediately lead to feelings of joy and peace. They don't just arrive the second you forgive someone. I wish! No. We need to invite Jesus in to heal us and bring that joy and peace.

I know all this is true because of what was about to happen in John's library. However, we will get to that in a second. First, I need you all to know that if you want to Enter Wild and you hold unforgiveness in your heart toward someone who hurt you, you will eventually have to forgive that person completely. Deep breath. I know it's hard to imagine. Oh but, friends, it's so worth it.

Here is a prayer I use when I need to forgive someone, which you will find useful in your journey as well. I find myself praying this nearly every other day, LOL.

> Father, it's obvious in Scripture that I must forgive in order to
> be in the family of God. You ultimately desire the freedom and
> healing that forgiveness brings to land on me. I choose to forgive
> everyone who has hurt me. I choose to forgive and release [insert
> specific name(s) here]. I release any judgment and punishment
> I have been anticipating in my heart, and I submit [insert specific
> name(s) here] and my unforgiveness to You. Holy Spirit, thank
> You for allowing forgiveness to invade my life. In Jesus's name,
> I pray. Amen!

The second type of forgiveness we need to seek is *our* forgiveness from God Himself. If you grew up in the church as I did, you heard about this every Sunday. God forgives our sins if we simply ask Him to. Although I appreciate the way my second-grade Sunday school teacher explained it to me, I think we sometimes confuse asking God for forgiveness with what truly needs to happen: repentance.

The act of repentance is quite simple. It's nothing more than coming to God to confess our sins with a heart of regret and a commitment to turn around and go God's way. But this means that you go in a direction that's completely opposite where your sin was taking you. THAT IS UP TO YOU. If you simply confess your sin and apologize to God but don't turn away from your sin, it is not repentance.

Repentance sometimes means paying a price, such as removing yourself from situations and setups that could draw you back into the sinful behavior or getting rid of certain possessions. It could mean eliminating certain relationships or avoiding places you used to hang out. The consequences of true repentance are RADICAL. It's obvious when someone has truly repented. Do you see how different this looks from a simple apology in a prayer? Apologizing to God for sinning is not the same as repentance. It's a step toward it, but it's not true repentance.

Remember 1 John 1:9? God's response to our repentance is forgiveness and cleansing. His response to our repentance is restoration. Freedom from guilt and shame.

Although all that is amazing news, I thought what I did when I left the confines of my marriage was unforgivable. I felt like my sin was far too great to be forgiven. Even though Heather forgave me, there were so many times I felt ashamed because I believed God was disappointed in me. Some of you have done things that you can't imagine God would forgive you for. I've got good news. You're wrong; no sin is too great. No amount of failure is too much. You may also be thinking, *I keep making the same mistake over and over!* Guess what? Just as God requires unconditional forgiveness of us, He also requires it of Himself.

I need you all to memorize this verse: "I, even I, am he who *blots out* your transgressions, *for my own sake,* and remembers your sins no more" (Isaiah 43:25, emphasis added).

Hold up! Did He just say for His own sake? The God who makes the earth spin and float wants to forgive my sins for HIS OWN SAKE? This is crazy talk. You see, God doesn't just want forgiveness so that *we* can be in relationship with Him. He wants forgiveness so that *He* can be in relationship with *us*. Mind. Blown. Our Father in heaven provides us forgiveness for the sake of relationship because HE IS THE ONE WHO WANTS IT.

When you have forgiven others, well, now it's time to ask God to forgive you.

Father God, thank You for allowing me the strength to forgive others. Now that I have done that, I come to You seeking Your forgiveness. I come to You by the blood of the Cross and power of the Resurrection to ask for Your forgiveness of all my sins. I take responsibility for [insert sins here] and for the iniquity that is in my heart, and I repent and begin to walk away from this sin. In the name of Jesus Christ, I pray. Amen.

Those first two areas of forgiveness are the ones that we hear about the most. And it's most often not forgiving others and not seeking God's forgiveness that keep us from freedom. But there is one more kind of forgiveness, which was *my* key to freedom. And I'm assuming it will be important for many of you as well. And that is forgiving self. If you have forgiven others and asked for God's forgiveness yet still don't feel free, you probably need to pursue self-forgiveness.

Many people won't even go here because they aren't taught how effective it is. If you are harboring bitterness against yourself, you are still in chains. Oftentimes, it takes someone else pointing out that we need to forgive ourselves. Which is why I found John. The good news for you is that maybe you don't need John. Maybe Carlitos is the one who, through my own story, will help you see if anything has been holding you back.

Remember the conversation I had with John about wanting "that part of me" to die or not wanting to come face to face with "that part of me" because I wanted to forget about it? Well, people, you probably know where this is going. Those are the parts of me that had been waiting years and years for this part of me to forgive them.

REFLECT AND PRACTICE

1. Who in your life are you currently harboring bitterness against?

2. What situation in your life do you need to ask God forgiveness for?

14

Me, Me, Me

I think that if God forgives us we must forgive
ourselves. Otherwise, it is almost like setting up
ourselves as a higher tribunal than Him.

C. S. LEWIS

"Carlos. Are you ready?"

"I think so," I said.

I'm not going to recount everything John and I prayed over the next few hours, but we began with an initial prayer so that I could invite Holy Spirit into the room and ask Him to remind me of a place where I felt close to Him. Immediately I visualized the mountains, which is where I feel most connected to God. I imagined I was sitting outside my tent next to a small mountain lake at ten thousand feet, helping Heather make dinner as the sun was beginning to set. Yep. That's exactly what I pictured. John began to ask me questions, such as where I saw Jesus in the scene. Until he asked me that, I actually didn't notice that Jesus was there. But He suddenly appeared behind the tent. He was in a hammock, just swinging back and forth. We continued exploring aspects of this imaginary scene, and at one point John asked me how I was feeling.

"So light. So, so LIGHT. That's the only way to describe it," I replied.

"Good. Good," John said. "That's what Jesus brings to us. Lightness. Breath. Peace. I just want you to stay there with Jesus and Heather for a few minutes."

I was totally fine with that. I could see this scene so clearly it was almost as if I were actually there.

As John led, I spent another thirty minutes or so visualizing and experiencing the presence of Jesus through this exercise. It was an incredible activity that grounded me for what was to come.

"Okay, Carlos. Now that we have spent some time in the presence of Jesus, I want you to ask Holy Spirit to remind you of a time when you absolutely did not feel His presence. I want you to ask Holy Spirit to recall for you a time when you felt void of the presence of God."

Wow, John. Quite an abrupt about-face. But okay, I'm game.

Before I could even begin to mouth the words asking Holy Spirit to direct me, an explosive memory popped into my head. I immediately felt nauseated. I was back in the condo where we lived when my marriage imploded. I saw myself reclining on our green sofa in the living room, my back toward the fireplace wall and my eyes facing the hallway. The hallway led toward the kids' bedrooms and the master bedroom. To my left, the kitchen opened onto a small dining area. It was a tiny condo with just one hallway connecting the three bedrooms. I had my laptop on my lap, and the house was dark. No lights were on. I saw myself smiling broadly, manically looking at my laptop and then checking to make sure that nobody was awake. It must have been two in the morning, which was my prime witching hour when I knew my family would be asleep and her family, on the West Coast, would also be asleep.

As soon as I saw this scene, my heart started racing and I began to panic. I immediately opened my eyes and stood up, coughing and holding my chest. I'm sure John thought I was having a heart attack.

"I'm sorry, John. That was really overwhelming, and now my heart is doing that thing again. I'm sorry. I think we may need to stop." I made eye contact with John, and he gave me that soft smile again.

He locked eyes with me and said softly, "By the blood of the Cross and the power of the resurrection of Jesus Christ, and with the authority given to me in His ascension, I command any foul spirits to leave this library. For this is my dominion, and they have no right to be here. Carlos, it's okay. We are close. This is why you are here. Sit, sit. Fear doesn't have a right in my home, and it's gone now."

He was right. It was gone. I took three deep breaths and sat back down.

"Close your eyes, Carlos. You don't have to be scared. What did you see? Where are you?"

So I told him. I told him in excruciating detail whom I was chatting with and the dark joy it brought me. I described the absolutely demented state of my mind. I was soon crying as I explained the state of my life at that point. A web of lies would soon bring disaster to my home. "I hate that guy. I don't even want to see him, John. He scares me. He's so, so sad. So lost," I said.

"It's okay, Carlos. I know it's so sad to see that part of you doing this. Tell me, Carlos, why does he scare you?" John asked.

Through my tears and snot and sweat and any other liquid that was gushing out of my face, I proceeded to tell John that I was scared he would come back and destroy my life again. I was scared he would use all that charm and charisma to do it again. He was literally intoxicated 24/7 with luck or alcohol or pride or something. He was always intoxicated.

"And do you know what that intoxication is doing for him, Carlos?" John continued. "It's protecting you from pain. As deranged as that sounds, and as unhealthy as it seems, that is what he is doing. He's simply trying to protect you from pain. And you know what that part of you needs? He needs forgiveness. Because you told me before that you no longer feel like the life of the party because you are so wrapped up in worry and fear. That the charm you used to have is gone. Well, let me tell you something, Carlos, the charm is not gone. You just left it with this part of you, and you have locked him away in a prison and thrown away the key. You don't have to be scared of him anymore. And to be honest, that part of you is more scared of you than you are of him. You are the one who has been judging, pitying, shaming him. He needs you to free him. With forgiveness."

Okay. At this point in the dialogue, you may be as weirded out as I was. Here John goes again, talking to me about me yet acting like the other me is really me but not me but is me. WHAT IS HAPPENING?

"Stay there, Carlos. Stay in that room. Where are you right now? Where are you watching this scene from?"

"I'm watching from the corner by the door," I answered.

"Okay. Good. Now I need you to understand something. Although you felt as if this was a time when you were completely separated from the love of God, that's actually not true. You were not separated from Jesus. Actually, He was in that room too. With you. Do you see Him, Carlos? Where is He?"

More emotion. More tears. I suddenly saw Jesus sitting behind me. He was holding me. "He's right behind me, John," I answered.

"What's He wearing? What does He look like?" John continued. He had me describe the image of Jesus that I hadn't initially seen. It was the same Jesus who was sitting in the hammock on that mountaintop. But now He was present in one of the darkest seasons in my life, holding me and caring for me amid addictions and affairs. He never left me.

So now I'm imagining this scene where I was on my laptop having an inappropriate relationship with someone who was not my wife. I see myself standing at the door watching, and I see Jesus behind me on the sofa holding my head. As he kept praying, John asked me to turn the light on in the room. Again, this was all happening in my mind as John led me through this visualization exercise. However, it seemed very real.

Then John said, "Carlos, see the part of you that was on the sofa? Would it be okay if you shut your laptop?"

Aloud I said yes, although I wasn't sure which me was responding.

"Carlos who is having the emotional affair, would it be okay if present-day Carlos sat down across from you?"

"Yes," I answered aloud again. It was surprisingly easy to not feel crazy while doing this absolutely crazy thing.

My eyes were still shut when John said, "Are you doing okay, Carlos?"

I knew he was talking to present-day Carlos who was sitting in the room with him. I opened my eyes and said yes. But he wasn't sitting where he had been before I closed my eyes. He was standing on my right now. Weird. "Carlos, I would like for you to imagine that Carlos-who-had-the-affair is in the open seat in front of you . . ."

I knew where this little charade was going. I had done this sort of thing before at Onsite. I was about to forgive affair-Carlos for the hurt and shame he brought to my family!

"Carlos, I would like you to ask the part of you that had the affair for your forgiveness," John continued.

Wait. What? I think he is confusing the versions of me. Why would present-day Carlos need to apologize to Carlos-who-had-the-affair? "But why? I didn't do anything?" I replied to John, with a whiney tone.

"Oh, but Carlos, you have. You have been judging, demeaning, accusing, pitying, and rejecting this part of you for far too long. You have shamed yourself, and you need to forgive yourself for that shame."

I closed my eyes, imagined myself sitting in the condo living room across from myself and went all in. "I'm so scared of you. I'm so scared to let you back into being a part of me. You destroyed my family. You destroyed my career. You destroyed the trust of my daughters. You did so much to harm me!" I was yelling at this point. "But I also know that you didn't know how to handle this. And you didn't know that Jesus, who you thought wasn't there, was sitting behind you as you made those medicating decisions. He was right there." My words were almost indistinguishable now. Just tears on tears on tears. "And Carlos-who-had-the-affair, I want to ask you if you will forgive me for shaming you all these years. And also, I forgive you for what you did to present-day me."

John chimed in, "Carlos, repeat this prayer after me . . ."

And this was the prayer that unlocked the prison door to the cell where I had been keeping this part of me. I type this out with the hope that you will use it as well to forgive the parts of yourself that you have held captive for far too long.

Father, because You have forgiven me, I choose to forgive myself
and to release myself from all judgments, accusations, hatred,
slander, mistakes, stupidity, and falling short of the mark. I choose
to accept myself as I am because You choose me as I am. I choose
to love myself again as You love me. I even expect to like myself
again. Holy Spirit, I ask You to work Your sanctification in me.
Change me into the image of Christ I know I can become. In the
name of Jesus Christ, I pray. Amen!

Friends. I know it's not magic, but the second I said amen, I felt something lift. I felt peace. I opened my eyes and smiled so big at John.

"We aren't done yet, Carlos. One more part of you."

John led me through a similar experience with the part of me I had been shaming for being anxious all these years. I had a whole conversation with the panic-ridden man I shamed for being so weak. And I brought that part of me back into relationship with Jesus as well. It was a long and grueling three hours in John's library, but when I finally opened my swollen eyes, John was crying as well.

"You did it, Carlos. Now you have a clear path toward abundance," he said.

Breakthrough

Let me reiterate that no part of forgiving ourselves is tied to our salvation. There is no Bible verse that directly tells us to forgive ourselves. However, there are plenty of principles in the Bible that do strongly encourage self-forgiveness. For instance, Mark 11:25 says, "And when you stand praying, if you hold anything against anyone, forgive them, so that your Father in heaven may forgive you your sins." "ANYONE" INCLUDES YOU.

I needed to forgive the part of me that made bad decisions that nearly destroyed my family, and he needed to forgive me. Because he was still a part of me. The part of me that was struggling daily with anxiety and panic? I needed to ask his forgiveness for judging and shaming him. This is so important for us to understand. It's not just about asking God to forgive us and forgiving others. We must also forgive ourselves. Since I forgave myself, I've experienced such profound freedom and release. The most amazing result? Those heart palpitations went away. They stopped. Like totally and completely stopped.

Are you reading this? A physical manifestation of my stress and anxiety DISAPPEARED when I forgave myself. Since that morning in John's library, I've seen dozens and dozens of other people freed through the power of self-forgiveness.

I had many more sessions with John. I kept finding more agreements I had made with lies, and I kept confessing those lies, rejecting them, and replacing the lies with God's truth. If I may borrow a line from my last book, I kept killing my spiders. Over and over again.

So much happened in my new friend's library in the subsequent years, enough to fill books that could cover the entirety of his library walls. But what you need to know for now is that the physical manifestation of my anxiety that had been plaguing me for eight months went away after two mornings with John.

We are carrying around in our bodies physical manifestations of the sin in our lives. But we don't have to anymore. Forgiveness is waiting to usher in a peace so WILD that you may just never go back to mild.

REFLECT AND PRACTICE

1. Is there anything for which you need to forgive yourself?

2. Look back at the situations and people you mentioned in the previous questions in this section (the chapters in part 2) and then take them to God by praying the prayer on the next page.

PAUSE AND PRAY

Father, Jesus, Holy Spirit,

I declare and proclaim that I belong to You, Jesus. I declare and proclaim that nothing else has claim over me. Jesus, I ask You to come into this area [insert answer from the end of chapter 7] that I am just coping with. I ask that You begin to reveal to me what abundance would look like for me in this area of my life.

I thank You for fulfilling the promise of [insert answer from the end of chapter 8] in my life, yet I confess that I find it hard to believe the promise that You will [insert answer from end of chapter 8] in my life. I reject the lie that I don't believe You will do it. And I replace that lie with the truth that [insert the scripture verse you chose to replace that lie].

Holy Spirit, I come to be restored and renewed in You in the areas of my life where I've been stuck. I confess that I don't believe I can be healed from [insert a behavior from end of chapter 9]. I renounce and reject that lie in the name of Jesus and send it to the foot of the Cross. I also confess the lie [insert lie you wrote at end of chapter 10], which has been producing the behavior keeping me back. I also confess to You, Jesus, that I've been judging the part of me that [insert answer from end of chapter 11]. I forgive myself for [insert answer from end of chapter 12]. I ask for that part of me to be restored and renewed in You, and I ask for that part of me to receive Your love, Your life, and all the grace and mercy it needs today. I bring that part of me back into relationship with all parts of me and ask You, Jesus, to seal all parts of me in Christ. I bring the Cross and the blood of Jesus Christ against anything that stands in the way of this reconciliation, and I receive the healing that You promise in Your Word.

Thank You for coming. Thank You for hearing my prayer. Thank You for healing me. In the name of Jesus, I pray. Amen.

PART III

ENTER WILD

15

I Doubt It

You will receive power when the Holy Spirit comes on you.

ACTS 1:8

I'm hoping you are seeing how all this connects:

- You can't Enter Rest without slowing down.
- You can't hear from God without first Entering Rest.
- You can't Enter War against a lie you don't know exists.
- You can't forgive someone else or yourself without first hearing from God what it is you need to forgive.

Now for the fun part. Once you win the war, you get to Enter Wild. You are now at a place where you can begin to step into the truth and wonder of our faith. This is what it's *really* supposed to look and feel like.

I want to let you know that it may not be like you imagined. Stepping into the land of miracles, signs, and wonders is not for the faint of heart or for those who want to do this Christianity thing only on the weekends. When you first experience WILD, you are going to want to tell all your friends about it. A few will believe you, but many won't. And you will look at them like, *Wait. Why would I lie to you? This is really happening. This is real.*

A video of Benny Hinn on YouTube shows him running around a stage in front of thousands of people, stretching his arms out to pray for people while they gracefully pass out into the arms of "catchers." There's a song playing called "Bodies" by some hard-core band named Drowning Pool, and you can hear the line "Let the bodies hit the floor."

I remember the day I saw that video.

It was the day I decided Holy Spirit was a joke.

It was the day I decided I wanted no part of that.

Give me a three-point sermon and a life hack.

Play some feel-good worship songs that give me goose bumps.

Give me scriptures that help me live a better life.

Give me a quiet, faraway God who will let me into heaven when I die.

But whatever you give me . . .

Don't give me that crazy Holy Spirit stuff.

Don't give me that spiritual warfare stuff.

Because it's gotta be fake. Seriously.

I know because I faked it once. I didn't mean to fake it . . . but I did.

Benny Hinn would have thought every last ounce of Holy Spirit power shot through his fingers and into my soul the way I fell back.

I was at my friend Brewster's little country church in backwoods Georgia somewhere. His dad was the pastor, and we were about to go on a mission trip. It was my first time attending his church, and when his dad called us up at the end of the service to pray for us, I thought nothing of it.

Everything was going fine until his dad started praying faster and then faster and faster, and then out of nowhere he came up to me and smacked me right in the forehead! I was so confused. Then he did it again. I can only imagine the look on my face. I had no idea what was going on.

Next, his dad walked away from me and toward Brewster, his prayers getting louder. I saw him pop Brewster in the head. AND LO AND BEHOLD, BREWSTER PASSED OUT!

Oh no. He's walking back toward me. Oh no! I thought.

Sure enough, Brewster's dad took my entire face in both of his hands. He stared at me square in the eyes and started praying like I've never heard anyone pray before. He shouted something and then popped me in the head with a force I'm assuming is intended only for Olympic volleyball action.

Down I went.

Down goes Whittaker.

Only I didn't pass out because I had been filled with some semblance of Holy Spirit. I passed out because Brewster passed out. I passed out because everyone was watching.

After church, after all the hugs and people saying "Go with God," Brewster and I found ourselves in a Sunday school room all alone. We didn't say anything to each other for at least thirty seconds. And then, almost in sync, we turned our heads and locked eyes.

"Did you fake it?" I asked. Silence.

"Did you fake it, man?" Silence.

"Brewster, did you fake it? Because I did and—"

Before I could finish talking, he said, "Yeah, man. I faked it. But don't tell my dad!"

And we started dying laughing.

We were laughing so hard, but something inside me, deep inside me, was sad. I wanted Brewster to tell me he didn't fake it. Because there was something incredibly wild about the whole experience. I'd never experienced anything like it with my conservative Baptist background.

When Brewster and I got to the airport, I could tell something was bothering him, so I asked, "You okay, man?"

"Carlos, I need to tell you something. I lied to you earlier. I was so nervous about you coming to church today with me. I know you weren't raised around anything like that. And when you asked me if I faked passing out, well, I lied. I lied because I didn't want you to think I was crazy. But the Holy Spirit has been pressing on my heart since we left church. I need to tell you. It's real. IT's ALL REAL," Brewster concluded.

I didn't say anything. I felt half relieved and half ashamed. *So there is something more to this faith I have been living?* I thought. *Something wild. But what is it? And how do I get it?*

Well, let me just tell you. Our friend John, with the piercing blue eyes and unapologetic silence, showed me what this sort of wild looked like. And the thing that relieved me most about what happened in John's library was that it was nothing like Benny Hinn. No hype. No body catchers. But what blew my mind was that it was crazier than anything I had ever experienced. (Honestly, that's not saying much coming from this former conservative Baptist evangelical.)

So as I said, people who have known you your entire lives may suddenly be skeptical of your newfound freedom and abundance. And how can we blame them? We were like them for so long. But what I've realized is that they just have to get a taste for themselves. Just. A. Taste. And that taste is all they need to follow your lead and Enter Wild.

This reminds me of the beginning of C. S. Lewis's book *The Lion, the Witch and the Wardrobe.* If you haven't read it, stick with me because I think it explains perfectly what I'm talking about when it comes to Entering Wild.

At the beginning of the story, we find that siblings Peter, Susan, Edmund, and Lucy Pevensie have been sent to the country to escape the air raids of World War II. They end up staying with a quirky old man named Professor Kirke, whose house is as quirky as he is. These children are living in the middle of a war. War is *normal* for them. They have grown used to it. But even in the midst of this war, they still have a childlike wonder.

The children begin to play hide-and-seek in this incredible house. Lucy, the youngest of the Pevensie clan, walks into an empty room to find a place to hide. She sees a massive wardrobe draped with dusty sheets and walks slowly toward it to pull the sheets off.

Into the wardrobe she goes. She leaves the wardrobe door cracked so that she can peek out of it. She slowly pushes through the collection of old fur coats toward the back of the wardrobe. She keeps backing up, and suddenly she feels a cold wind blowing over her shoulders and realizes snow is falling too. She turns around and stares into a magical land that should not exist at the back of a closet. Surely she must be dreaming. It is beautiful and it looks so real. Her face lights up as she walks through the snow under the canopy of pines and catches snowflakes in her hand. What in the world is this magical place?

After exploring for what seems like hours, she runs back through the wardrobe to find her siblings and tell them what she has experienced. And guess what? THEY DON'T BELIEVE HER. They don't. They think her imagination is running wild.

We've seen this before in the gospel stories. Jesus's best friends were frequently skeptical. Daily. Jesus often said, "O you of little faith." Not "O you of massive faith." No. His disciples, the ones who would take His word to all the earth, those guys were so filled with doubt. The night of the Last Supper, Jesus told them that He would meet them in Galilee after His resurrection. "Then the eleven disciples went to Galilee, to the mountain where Jesus had told them to go. When they saw him, they worshiped him; but some doubted" (Matthew 28:16–17). Do you see that? They doubted *after* Jesus appeared to them.

Although they heard it from Jesus Himself, and they were witnessing firsthand exactly what He told them He would do, *some still doubted*.

Before I stepped into the wild side of abundance, I definitely identified with the doubting disciples. Even though they had traveled and ministered with Jesus for years and seen hundreds of miracles, signs, and wonders firsthand, they still doubted. Oh, the humanity! It honestly makes me feel so much better about pre-abundance Carlitos. And honestly, even seeing

Jesus show up so clearly in my day-to-day life, even after I have seen the miracles and wonders, I STILL FIND MYSELF DOUBTING. We are only human, just as the disciples were. And your friends, the ones who doubt your newfound abundance in this Holy Spirit–filled life, they aren't bad friends. They aren't mean. Some may even be trying to protect you.

Let's go back to the Pevensies for a second. Lucy tells her siblings about the world she discovered, which was called Narnia. They don't believe her. Not only that, but they are legitimately worried about their sister. So they go and seek some wisdom from Professor Kirke.

They tell him that their sister's imagination has run wild and that she thinks there is a forest in the back of the wardrobe. After Lucy's older siblings express their skepticism and belief that Lucy must be lying or worse, crazy, Professor Kirke responds:

> Madness, you mean? Oh, you can make your minds easy about that. One has only to look at her and talk to her to see that she is not mad. . . . There are only three possibilities. Either your sister is telling lies, or she is mad, or she is telling the truth. You know she doesn't tell lies and it is obvious that she is not mad. For the moment then and unless any further evidence turns up, we must assume that she is telling the truth.[21]

I can't think of a better scene to depict what happens in our lives when we Enter Wild.

So whether you are like Lucy and have already stepped through the wardrobe or you are like Thomas who saw Jesus and still wasn't convinced or maybe you're like Peter and Susan and you're worried about your friend Carlos, thinking maybe I've just gone mad . . .

I ask you to do nothing, as I take you by the hand . . .

And let me show you this new land of abundance.

Then you can decide for yourself if you want to stay where you are or not.

You ready? Let's go.

REFLECT AND PRACTICE

1. What is the hardest thing to believe about the miraculous side of your faith? Write it down.

2. When was the last time you saw God do something WILD? Describe it here.

16

Redneck Thai

When he brings all his sheep out, he goes ahead
of them, and they follow him because they know
his voice.

JOHN 10:4, NCV

We were created to hear the voice of God. This gets to become a
normal thing for you, because this is where Entering Wild begins. But
when we begin to see God move in miraculous ways, we can get to the
point where we are looking only for the big things. When I Entered Wild
I was walking around like I was ready to raise someone from the dead in
the name of Jesus. I wanted to part the Red Sea. I wanted to experience
these huge breakthroughs and see God do amazing things through me.
Although I believe God can use a human being like me to do massive
things, the small things are just as miraculous as the big ones. I promise.
When you first step into Wild, start small. Yep. That's right. Don't go trying to raise someone from the dead right off the bat.

I have a friend named Alex. We've been friends for a long time, since we grew up in the same church where we learned the same Bible stories. We were even on staff at the same church for a period of time. So Alex knew my theology and had walked alongside me as I matured in my faith. But when Heather started showing me how I was supposed to hear from God, my faith began to accelerate at a different speed than Alex's. Not a better pace, just a different pace.

I'll never forget when Alex texted me about a year into this new WILD way of life. I still have his text on my phone:

"Los. Hey, man. So listen. I've been really trying to hear the voice of God lately. I know you have got Him tuned in and I was wondering if maybe you could help me? Coffee this week?"

I responded immediately: "How about now?"

Thirty minutes later, we were sitting inside Crema, one of my favorite coffee shops in Nashville. We were sitting at a small table in the back of the café next to the giant garage door.

"Okay, Los. So, man, I've been trying. But I just can't seem to do it. I know Jesus loves me. I know that the Holy Spirit is supposed to guide me, but I CAN'T HEAR ANYTHING. Am I doing it wrong? Help me."

I smiled and immediately responded, "You are about to hear God. Like right now. You are going to hear Him. Are you ready?"

He looked at me like I was crazy, almost in disbelief. No, definitely in disbelief. I think he thought I was going to suggest a book to read, or a sermon to listen to. I don't think he thought I was going to say, "Right now you will hear." But I did and he didn't know how to feel about it.

"Wait a second, man. Like right now? You are telling me that right now I'm going to hear God?"

"Absolutely," I replied. My steadfast confidence that he was about to hear the voice of God was making Alex *super* uncomfortable. It was funny.

"Like right now? I'm gonna hear Him?" He still was not believing me.

"Yes, man. RIGHT NOW. You ready?"

He nodded without saying anything, as if he didn't want to mess things up. "Mmm hmm," he managed to say.

"Okay, man. This isn't complicated. Don't make it more difficult than it is. Holy Spirit is talking to us all the time. I want you to ask God where you and I should go to lunch."

He got that look on his face, the look a friend gives you when you dare them to do something that you know they are not going to do. Like *You are crazy if you think I am going to eat that live scorpion.* That was the look he gave me.

"Really? *Really?* You want me to ask God where you and I should go to lunch? You really think God is going to answer that? That seems a little silly, don't you think?"

"Alex. Do you think God cares about the big things in life?"

"Of course."

"So do you think He also cares about the little things?"

"Yes," he replied.

"Great. So now we are on the same page. God is going to talk to you not only about the massive things but also about the small things. And I'd be willing to bet most of His talking to us is about the small things anyway. Learn to hear Him in the small things, and you will be able to hear Him more clearly in the big ones."

"But how am I going to hear Him? Will it be an audible voice? Like I'm hearing your voice now? Will it be an energy? Will it be in my head? In my heart?" Alex was getting freaked out now.

"Just relax, man," I told him.

As you can see, sometimes we make this out to be much weirder than it actually is. Again, this is normal stuff, friends. WILD. But normal.

When I was growing up in the eighties, watching television was way different than it is today. In those days, the stations would broadcast signals through the sky and we needed an antenna to be able to tune in. You never assumed that the station wasn't broadcasting. It always was. But it was up to us to tune into the signal correctly. So if a game was on ABC, and we turned to channel 2, it didn't mean we could automatically see the game. No. We had to adjust the antennas, until finally, after dancing with them, wrapping foil around them, leaning them against each other, we got a clear enough signal. Then we could sit back and enjoy the broadcast. BUT NOT UNTIL WE DID SOME WORK FIRST.

Hearing from God is much the same. Holy Spirit is speaking; we just have to be able to tune in.

So begrudgingly Alex accepted the challenge. He looked at me, interlaced his fingers, put his elbows on the coffee-shop table, then looked up and slowly said, "Dear God, or Jesus, or whoever is listening right now, can you please tell me where Carlos and I should go to lunch?" Then he looked back at me, as if waiting for some sort of thumbs-up. After about fifteen seconds, he looked back up into the rafters of Crema and said a little bit louder, "Amen." As if maybe that would be the necessary connection to heaven.

I let my boy sit there in discomfort for an entire minute. He kept looking at me, then looking up. Then he would look around. He stuck his fingers in his ears a few times. He picked up his phone after forty-five seconds, then put it back down. I don't know; maybe he thought God was gonna text him? He was fidgeting. He was super uncomfortable.

Finally, I let him off the hook. "So, man? Anything? Did you hear anything?"

"No, MAN! I mean, I don't think so? I don't know. I didn't hear any words. Ugh. I don't know. I told you this wasn't going to work," he said in defeat.

"Not so fast, Alex. Did you feel anything? Did anything surface in your mind?" I asked.

"Oh, now we are talking about *feelings*? Everybody has feelings, Carlos. I knew you were going to say that. Feelings. How do I know if my feelings are me or God? How do I know what's Him?"

I stopped him. "Alex. Don't edit the Holy Spirit. We have a tendency to do that all the time. When you asked God where we were supposed to go to lunch, what did you see? What did you hear? What did you feel?"

His eyes got bigger.

"What is it? What? I knew you heard something!"

"Well. Man. I don't know."

"No, Alex. You do know. I can see it in your eyes. What did you see? Don't be scared. You can say it."

Friends, here is where we find ourselves so many times. You see, I knew Alex saw something. I could see it in his eyes. But he didn't want to say it because HE DIDN'T WANT TO BE WRONG. This right here. This is the point in our conversational intimacy with Jesus where we give up. We are scared to be wrong. And I get it. I mean if we don't hear correctly, then suddenly we can have a crisis of faith. So instead we stay safe and shallow in our prayers. But that will never get us into abundance.

"Say it, Alex. Just say it." I knew he heard or saw something. I could tell.

"Well, man, I don't know. I don't wanna say it because, was it me or God? Maybe it was just my stomach talking?"

When Heather calls me, I know it's her. Not only because it says so on my phone's screen, but because I know the sound of her voice. I have heard it for twenty years. The same is true with the voice of God. The more time we spend listening, the more we are going to know His voice.

"Say it, Alex."

"Well, when I said amen, I suddenly saw in my mind that Thai restaurant over in the Tennessee Titans stadium parking lot. Thai Phooket. You know that place? That's what I saw. But was it God?"

I immediately interrupted him. "Let's go, man. Let's go where God told us to go eat lunch."

And off we went.

We had an incredible lunch at Thai Phooket. It was so delicious. But guess what? Jesus didn't appear in my Thai chicken curry soup. The server didn't walk out levitating a copy of the Ten Commandments. Nothing magical happened at all. It was a nice, normal lunch. In fact, by the end of lunch we had actually forgotten that we had asked God where we should go eat. We paid the bill and walked outside. We walked over to our respective vehicles, which were parked next to each other. Alex got on his motorcycle, and I opened the door to my minivan (different seasons of life, friends). "See you ma—"

Before I could say goodbye, we heard screaming coming from Thai Phooket. It startled us both, and we turned our heads to see what was happening. A man was sprinting toward us, like full-on sprinting.

I need you to imagine the biggest redneck you have ever seen. Now multiply his or her redneckness by ten. That was the man who was now yelling something at us. We couldn't make it out until he was about twenty feet away.

"Hey, man! Hey! Hey, man! Hey, you!" The closer he got, the crazier he looked. "Hey! You man." He was pointing at Alex. "Hey, man, listen. You are gonna think I'm crazy. You guys are going to think I'm crazy, man. Hey, man, you are going to think—"

Alex interrupted, "YES. WE THINK YOU ARE CRAZY. What's up?"

"You are gonna think I'm crazy, man, but listen. Do you sometimes work on your laptop over at that coffee shop called the Frothy Monkey? Over on 12th Avenue?" he asked Alex.

"Um, yeah."

"Well, man, listen. You are gonna think I'm crazy, but I was in there the other day. I was reading my Bible and you walked in. As soon as you walked in, I felt something in my gut tell me to walk up to you and pray for you. But I didn't 'cause that's weird and creepy, right? So I ignored that and kept doing what I was doing, never thinking I would see you again. But then, I was just sitting here at Thai Phooket sipping on my soup and minding my own business and YOU CAME WALKING IN! I nearly spit out my soup! And there was the prompting again. I needed to pray for you. But I let you walk out again. And when you left, I felt Holy Spirit tell me that I can't let you leave twice.

"So I got up and chased you, man, and listen, I know it sounds crazy. But can I please pray for you?"

Alex's mouth was hanging open so wide you could have parked the *Titanic* in there.

I got in my minivan and left Alex in that parking lot all alone with that crazy redneck. But I was smiling so big as I drove off and saw that man's hand on Alex's shoulder as he prayed aloud.

Alex called me ten minutes later. With a voice that trembled, all he said was, "God answered my specific question! Carlos, GOD ANSWERED!" His prayer life has never been the same.

So often, we miss hearing God because we are waiting for some massive revelation and God wants to give us simple instructions. If we disobey or don't hear His prompting in the small things, why in the world would He give us the big things?

That's why Jesus told us to become like little children, which means not to be high minded and think we know it all. To tune into God's frequency, you must be willing to hear His voice in the small things.

He called a little child to him, and placed the child among them. And he said: "Truly I tell you, unless you change and become like little children, you will never enter the kingdom of heaven. Therefore, whoever takes the lowly position of this child is the greatest in the kingdom of heaven." (Matthew 18:2–4)

It's not complicated. Ask. Hear. Ask. Hear. Ask. Hear.
Wild is waiting!

REFLECT AND PRACTICE

1. Choose a seemingly insignificant thing to pray about, and ask
   God for direction.

2. After He answers you, follow through with the prompting you
   felt and write it down.

17

Googling God

All Scripture is God-breathed and is useful for
teaching, rebuking, correcting and training in
righteousness, so that the servant of God may
be thoroughly equipped for every good work.

2 TIMOTHY 3:16–17

If there was a Nobel Prize for "sticking around while your husband
heals the parts of his heart that need healing even though it is taking longer than paint does to dry," we all know Heather would have won this
award five years running. I am seriously so blessed. And after a few rounds
in John's library, I was finally in a place to reciprocate.

You see, I grew up in a culture where it was preached Sunday after
Sunday that the *man* should be the spiritual leader of his family. And let
me tell you, that may be the most confusing statement in the history of
confusing church statements.

Does that mean I'm supposed to pray more than she does?

Does that mean I'm supposed to read my Bible more than she does?

Is it a competition?

But Heather loves Beth Moore Bible studies way more than I do. So, is providing financially considered spiritual leadership? Is it spiritual leadership to take out the trash before she asks me to? What about Scripture memory? Because she can basically quote the entire Bible.

On and on my questions went. I felt like a failure in the "spiritual leader" department. I felt like we were running a marathon and Heather got a twenty-two-mile head start. There was no way I could catch her.

"Babe. I don't know how I will ever catch up with you. You have been walking with God and living this Wild life for so much longer than I have. How in the world am I ever supposed to lead you if I can't even catch up with you?"

"Babe. It's not a race. I'm not your competition. I *want* to follow you. I *want* to be led by you. Like, just do it. Lead me right now. The next decision you make, make it with all of us in mind and with His direction. With that one decision, you will be leading not just me, but Sohaila, Seanna, and Losiah as well." She sounded so matter of fact as she said this.

Okay, sounds easy enough. So do you know what I did after finally Entering Wild? Instead of doing exactly what she said, I went to Google. I googled "How to be a godly husband." Isn't that just like us? We have access to the God who makes the earth spin, and we go instead to find an expert we don't need to tell us something we don't know. When in reality we have access to the Expert of all experts, to God Himself.

I found a sermon from 1998. Now, there is NOTHING WRONG with sermons from 1998. But why in the world would I do that instead of simply pressing into the heart of God? I'll tell you why. Because I didn't trust my ability to hear God the way Heather did. Where is my handy list of five ways to lead my wife spiritually? I finally found a list after clicking off the sermon.

But the article I read told me three ways to lead, by demonstrating, deciding, and delegating. Um. No offense to the author of this article, but

I'm fairly certain that leading my wife isn't supposed to be narrowed down to three words that start with the same letter. This was going downhill fast. WHY IS GOOGLE FAILING ME NOW?!

This is how so many of us live our faith, just as we do all the other areas of our lives. We trust Google more than God.

Not long after I finally found freedom through forgiveness, Heather, the kids, and I moved into a new home in Nashville. It was the first home we'd lived in since moving to this great city. We had been in a condo for five years, and it felt good to finally have some more room for our growing family. This may sound silly, but I was really looking forward to having next-door neighbors. I had spent my condo years imagining having a cold beer with my neighbor after both of us mowed our yards on Saturday mornings. I know that sounds cheesy, like I would be living on the perfect cul-de-sac in the perfect neighborhood in 1982, before people stopped hanging out with one another and started staring at their phones 24/7. I had been praying for this version of my best life. And guess what? I got it. I GOT THE PERFECT NEIGHBOR. His name was Bill.

Bill was a lawyer in his fifties, his wife was a teacher, and their kids were in college. They had two dogs, a cat, one chicken, a garden in the backyard, and a nicely kept front lawn. They brought cookies over the day we moved in. He took me over to his house and gave me a tour after I gave him a tour of my house.

"Carlos, we are so glad you guys moved in. This neighborhood has needed some kids in it for a long time. Betty and I were talking last night about how nice it is to hear your kids playing on the trampoline. Makes us miss ours but sure is nice to have some life on the street."

We walked through his house, and he introduced me to all his pets. His dogs, Larry and Larry (I don't get it either); his cat, Garfield; and his pet chicken, Stella. Yes. His chicken had a name. It was weird but also kinda cute, so whatever.

"So your chicken has a name? Like it's not just for laying eggs?"

"Oh, Stella quit laying eggs a long time ago. When all the other chickens died, we decided to make Stella a pet! I let her out twice a day, and she follows me around everywhere I go. I know. It makes me the weird middle-aged man in the neighborhood, but it's worth it. I love that chicken. How about you? What are your pets named?"

"Henry is our cat, and Pope is our dog. Henry is mean. I'm sorry, but just ignore him. And Pope? Well, he may be the gentlest 120-pound dog in the history of big dogs. Wanna meet him?"

So I took Bill over to the house, and he and Pope became fast friends. Listen, my dog is the dog of the decade. Trust me. He's kinda a diva. He hates it outside. He lives inside. He's a purebred Bernese Mountain Dog with eyes that would melt the hardest of hearts. (Actually, you can go look him up on Instagram right now: @thedogpope. You're welcome.) Heather had wanted this breed of dog her whole life. She flew to Virginia to pick him up, and she loved him with everything. After Bill cuddled with Pope and was hissed at by Henry, he went back home.

"Can you believe we lucked out and got the neighbor of the century?" I asked Heather.

"I'm glad you got your beer-drinking lawn-mower neighbor, Carlos. Now can you finish helping me unpack?" Oops.

The first fourteen days in our new home were everything we imagined they would be. Lots of eating with plastic spoons and knives. Lots of ignoring this box and that box. Lots of figuring the ins and outs of our new environment. And lots of Bill. We had at least a five-minute conversation by the fence every day about life, liberty, and justice. Or at least about the weather. And, yes, Stella the chicken was always by his side.

On day fifteen, I was about five miles from home around two o'clock on a Saturday afternoon. I honestly can't remember what I had been doing, but I do remember I was driving in my Jeep when I got the phone call. I saw my daughter Seanna's name on the phone, and I picked it up.

She was screaming, "Daddy! DADDY! Come home now. Come home fast. Please hurry! You have to come home *now*!"

All blood immediately drained from my face and traveled into my feet. My heart began to race. The terror in her voice was palpable. She was undone about something. Immediately, I feared the worst. Something horrible had happened to one of her siblings. Or to her mom.

"Baby. Seanna. Calm down and talk to Daddy. I'm coming home. I just need you to tell me calmly what's wrong. Did something happen to Losiah? Sohaila? Mommy? Tell me what's wrong so I can help." I was actually quite amazed at how calm I was in the moment. Because everything inside me told me I was about to hear the worst news of my life. "Seanna, WHAT HAPPENED? What's wrong with them?" I repeated.

"Daddy! NOTHING is wrong with them! They are fine, Daddy!" More tears. More hyperventilating. Okay. To be honest, everything inside my spirit immediately settled when she told me that. Why? Because although I loved Pope, if something happened to him, I knew we could get past that with some work. I knew we would mourn. *But at least it's not one of my humans.* "Oh, baby. Okay then. Tell me what's wrong. I'm almost home now." I was probably two minutes away now.

"Daddy, it's Pope," she said.

There it was. I knew it! *Okay. We can get through this. I know it will be hard, but we will get past it. I wonder if he got hit? I wonder if he's still alive?* "Baby, what's wrong with Pope?" I pressed.

"Dad! NOTHING is wrong with Pope! Pope is in trouble! Daddy, Pope is running around the yard, and Mr. Bill's Stella is hanging out of his mouth. Daddy . . . Pope killed Stella!"

Oh no.

No.

Not the perfect neighbor's beloved pet chicken! No! *How in the world?* This was terrible news. *What am I going to do?* "Put your mom on the phone," I told Seanna.

She handed the phone to Heather. I couldn't even get a word in before Heather said, "You need to come home now, and tell your neighbor that your dog killed his chicken!"

Oh, I see how it is. Suddenly this dog, the one my wife had dreamed about getting her entire life while I didn't even want a dog, had suddenly gone from being *her* dog to *my* dog.

"Okay, babe. I'm thirty seconds from home."

What in the world was I going to do? How was I going to tell the neighbor of the year that his beloved Stella had died in the jaws of my dog of the year? How was I going to tell him? And how did it happen? UGH. I did not want to pull in the driveway. I did not want to face Bill. I was racking my brain for something to say. So I did what any dad in his late thirties would do when I pulled in the driveway.

I pulled out my phone and I googled: "What to tell your neighbor when your dog kills their chicken." Dead serious. I googled it. And guess what? Fourteen pages. Fourteen glorious pages of search results came flooding onto my phone. I spent three minutes quickly scouring the endless pages of backyard chicken forums. And the number one thing I realized is, *Wow, people really love their chickens.*

But the second, and most important, thing I discovered was this: if you are more sad about your neighbor's chicken than he is . . . he will forgive you.

Seriously, every single page I read said that. All of them. Well, for a fairly dramatic man like myself, that should come fairly easily.

So I got out of my car and slowly made my way across my lawn to Bill's lawn and then slowly up to his front door. *Be sad, Carlos. Be sad,* I kept thinking. *Be very sad about Stella.* I even tried thinking about some really sad memories that would make me tear up. But every time I tried to get sad about Stella the chicken, all my brain kept telling my heart was that it was just a stupid chicken. Chickens aren't even supposed to have names. I couldn't for the life of me get sad. UGH.

I rang Bill's doorbell. *C'mon, Carlos. Get sad. Please produce just one single Denzel tear to drip down your face. Just one.*

The door opened and there stood Bill, just as energetic as he is every time I see him. "Carlos! Hey, man! Come on in! My three boys just got home from college! Come inside and meet them. I'm so glad you stopped—"

I stopped him before he could continue. "John, hey, man. Now may not be the best time." *Get sad, Carlos. C'mon man. Get sad.* "I have some bad news. You see, Pope got out of the house. He never gets out of the house. I don't know how that happened. But apparently Stella was out of her coop as well, and—there's no easy way to say this, Bill. I'm so sorry, Bill, but Pope killed Stella. I think he thought she was a toy. I'm so SAD, Bill. I'm so sorry. Is there anything I can do? Can I buy you another chicken? Where do people buy chickens anyway? Bill, I'm so sorry."

Bill uttered only one word as he raised his left fist to his mouth and bit it while his eyes welled up with tears. "Stella?"

Oh man. He was crying. This was going south fast. *C'mon, Carlos. Get sad! C'mon!* "Bill. I'm so sorry man. I'm so sad about it." Maybe if I *told* him I was sad, he would believe me.

"Where is Stella now?" he asked.

Before I could respond, I heard a commotion behind me. It was Heather. And she looked visibly shaken up. As she walked up the stairs, I realized . . . SHE WAS REALLY CRYING. She was actually sad.

"Bill?" Heather said. "Bill, I'm so sorry." She. Was. Crying. Crying real tears over this chicken. And then something happened that changed my perspective on Google once and for all. The second Heather shed her first tear, Bill's tears disappeared. Truly. He looked at Heather, and three seconds later he said, "It's okay, Heather. It's in a dog's nature. They are predators at heart. It's okay. He's not a bad dog. We will be fine. A little sad but fine." And he kept talking and talking, but all I could think was, *It worked! Google worked!*

Friends. Amigos. Amigas. How often are we living our faith like this? We are googling the answers to our faith and testing out every possible method to living it out. Crossing our fingers and holding our breath with every single situation we come across. Googling how to stop drinking. How to stop looking at porn. How to fix our relationships. How to [fill in the blank].

It's incredible how often we bypass the power of the Holy Spirit only to grab onto the power of something else. ANYTHING ELSE. We don't need to operate like this! We don't need Google when we have the living and active Word of God. We don't need podcasts when we have the voice of God Himself.

Listen. I'm not saying that we don't occasionally need help from our friends or from other sources. Of course we do. But what I am saying is we will never, ever Enter Wild if we keep bypassing the wildness of the Holy Spirit. It won't happen. We have access to the full abundant life promised in His Word.

So I put my phone down, went into my bedroom, and fell on my knees.

> Father God, I've come so far. I know all the tools. I know I'm free.
> So why is it so hard to believe I can lead my family into this wild
> and free season of abundance? Lord, I confess the lie that I can't
> lead my family because of my past sin. I reject that lie and replace
> it with the truth that I am the leader of my household and I will
> lead them closer to You. So, Jesus, kind Savior, please tell me what
> direction we should go as a family. Please show me, Lord, how to
> lead them. Amen.

I felt as if a weight had been lifted off my shoulders. I felt physically lighter. Okay. Now what? I listened. God responded and His voice was so loud. *Your identity is not in being a worship leader. It's time to stop singing and start speaking.*

I wish I could describe the clarity of what I felt and heard. At the same time, I thought it was insanity. I was signed with a major record label. I was touring with the biggest names in Christian music. And God wanted me to STOP SINGING and START SPEAKING? *This is obviously not from the Lord,* I thought. So I did what we *all* should do when we hear something that doesn't sit right with us. I checked it against Scripture and with people I trusted who also walk with God.

One at a time, my friends all confirmed that I'd heard from God. One of my friends, Mike Foster, even went so far as to say, "Carlos. You are a thought leader. People read your blog not because you write pretty songs but because they want to learn from you. You have been blogging for years. It's time to transform into the person they already know you are."

Nope. Next.

Then I remembered a conversation I had with Andy Stanley during my last weeks at North Point Community Church in Atlanta. "Carlos, the reason you are a great worship leader isn't because you have a great voice. No. It's because when you walk out onstage, within five seconds everyone in the room is on your side. They feel like they are your best friend. You can't teach that to people. You just have it or you don't. And you have it."

One conversation after another kept confirming what I had heard from the Lord. When I asked Heather, she didn't even bat an eyelid. "Yes. That's what you should be doing. You will always be able to lead worship, but that's not what's next for you. Write books and talk about them. God is right."

Friends, I ignored God's prompting and the words of my friends for six months. I was scared to death of leaving the safety of what I knew, my identity, for the wilderness of something new. Then finally, six months after I felt that call from God, I opened my laptop and did something that nobody should ever advise you to do. I quit my job. I emailed everyone who had booked me as a worship leader and told them I was now transitioning into being a speaker. I said I would no longer take worship-leading opportunities but if any of them needed a speaker for their church or event, I was now their guy.

There was only one problem with that.

I wasn't their guy.

What happened next looked less like WILD and more like wilderness.

Sometimes God is going to ask you to do some big and crazy things.

REFLECT AND PRACTICE

1. In what area of your life have you been intentionally avoiding asking God to move because you are scared of His answer?

2. In what area of your life have you heard God clearly but are ignoring His call?

18

The President

Your ways, God, are holy.
    What god is as great as our God?
You are the God who performs miracles;
    you display your power among the peoples.

PSALM 77:13–14

At this point in my story, most of the massive agreements I'd made with lies in my life had been destroyed. I say most because we are always on the hunt for our spiders. That process never ends. But once the spiders die, abundance begins. After I watched my wife step into Wild and learn to hear from God, then embarked on a massive spider hunt with John in his library and found freedom through forgiveness, I was beginning to see our wild, incredible God show up in miraculous ways on a daily basis. EVERY SINGLE DAY.

I began asking for mini-miracles regularly. These "coincidences" stopped being coincidences after about a week. At one point, I remember laughing and thinking, *This stuff can't be happening. I have to be on the greatest lucky streak in the history of the universe.* I say that because I asked

God simple and specific questions and He answered them in *dramatic* ways. The only way I can describe it is that it was as if God kept taking my simple questions and sprinkling some glitter on His answers.

One day I asked God if I should go left instead of right pulling out of the kids' school. I know. Sounds dumb. But this is the simple stuff I'm talking about. I asked Him, "Should I go downtown to write? Or should I go to Brentwood?" Brentwood was left. Downtown was right. I heard left. But I turned right because I wanted to work at Crema, my favorite coffee shop. I drove about a hundred yards and felt strongly I was supposed to turn around. Ugh. I really wanted to go to Crema.

I pulled a U-turn right in the middle of Franklin Road. "Okay, I'll go this way, God. Where do You want me to go?" I prayed.

I heard, *The Well.* Ugh. No. Nothing against that particular coffee shop, but it's as crowded as the DMV at noon and the tables shake when I type. (What can I say, I type *really hard*. My poor keyboard.) So I headed toward the suburban café. As soon as I turned left on Old Hickory, I felt another strong prompting.

I sensed that I needed to text a friend I hadn't talked to in a very long time. Our relationship had become strained, and it was soon clear why God had me turn around. He worked in the office building where the Well Coffeehouse was located. I hadn't spoken to him in over eight months. He had hurt me and I was bitter. Now I felt very keenly that not only was I supposed to go to the coffee shop with the wobbly tables, but I was supposed to text my buddy Pete too.

At the red light I texted him. "Hey, man. I'm heading to the Well. I think it's at the office complex where you work. I'd love to hug your neck if you are around . . . No pressure. But just felt led to reach out."

Not ten seconds later I see the little text bubbles pop up on my phone. You know the ones that pop up when the other person is typing something but you can't see what they're typing.

Also, don't you hate it when you see those bubbles and then they disappear? You know the person you're texting with typed something and then deleted it! I hate it. I think I have a complex. Anyway, back to the convo.

When his text appeared, it said, "CARLOS! YES! You are not going to believe this. I need to see you. Like right now. Are you there yet? I'll come meet you!"

Wow. That was a bit extra. Also, Pete normally takes a week to respond to texts. *Okay, God. I see You.*

Thirty seconds later I pulled into the parking lot. I saw Pete in the window. Wow. It was good to see his face. I walked in and we embraced. Then he shared something that made my jaw drop.

"Carlos. This is crazy. Listen. I've been wanting to write you and Heather an email apologizing. I've wanted to write you for a long time. But I didn't . . . until today. Carlos, look at this email."

He pulled out his phone and showed me a half-written email.

"I was literally halfway through this email to you and Heather . . . and your text came through. To be honest, it freaked me out a little bit. That's why I sprinted down here. You don't have spies watching me, do you?" He laughed.

I laughed. We had an incredible time. Knowing that it was ordained just made it that much better.

When I got back in the minivan, I just smiled and looked up. "I should have turned left to start with. I know better now." And I went north toward downtown . . . to the café I initially wanted to write in. Now I could.

Friends, this is what I'm talking about. The small stuff. And this stuff—it's happening EVERY DAY! I know people think I'm nuts as I wander through airports now, mumbling to God as if He's standing right next to me. What they don't know is that He is! And He is also right there beside you. Right now. He's ready for you to Enter Wild. Small things lead to the big things, just as I was saying at the end of the last chapter. Heather wanted me to begin to talk to God not just about which way to turn but about the big things too, such as decisions that would define the future of our family.

And I did. And then I ignored Him. And then I didn't. And then . . .

After I sent the email to cancel all my bookings, I shut my laptop and stood up with breath in my lungs. I had *never* been this obedient after receiving such clear direction from God. I was a very successful worship leader at the time. I was booked to lead worship around the country for months on end. We were turning people away every week. I couldn't keep up with the demand. And to think I had just decided to stop taking worship-leading requests because God told me to start speaking . . . Nobody can say I didn't jump in headfirst. I walked out of the bedroom so proud of myself and trusting God completely. I knew He would provide.

I just knew that every single person I emailed would email me back that day with the following message: "Hey, Carlos! Wow! This is amazing. Thanks for following the prompting of the Spirit. You know what? We want you to come and preach at our next event. If God told you so, He told us so!"

I went to bed with such swagger. Heather was visibly proud of me as well. She never worries. It's ridiculous how steadfast she is.

I woke up bright and early and grabbed my phone to check my emails. Not only had none of the church or conference teams emailed me back telling me how proud they were of me, none of them had asked me to speak either. But I did get a few emails saying, "Good luck!"

Then the word began to spread, and I put it on social media. People began hitting me up saying things like, "Are you sure that was God? Are you sure, Los? That seems a bit risky. Like this is not a game. This is your family."

One day turned into three. Three days turned to seven. I heard nothing. No interest.

My calendar was quickly emptying and nothing was filling it back up. *God, what have I done?*

A week turned into ten days. And ten became thirteen. And I'll never forget the conversation I had with God on day thirteen. Honestly, my side was filled with more curse words than Scripture. I was so mad. Why had He let me down? Or had it really been Him speaking at all? Ugh. Failure. I was losing influence, not gaining it. This was so backward. What had gone wrong?

Day fourteen. Fourteen days of nobody asking me to say a word, not a single speaking request. Nobody was even asking me to sing. Because I told them I was done with that, I had taken that opportunity off the table. At about two o'clock in the afternoon, I walked over to my laptop and opened it up. I opened up Gmail and started typing an email to a few churches I had contacted previously. "Dear _____. Hey. Listen. So I think I may have jumped the gun a little bit. I know I asked you to take me off the schedule but . . ." Then I stopped.

No. This wasn't right. I was about to do what my human nature wanted me to do. I was about to hustle my way out of the mess instead of letting God carry me through the mess. So I did what I knew I needed to do.

I hit Delete.

Three hours after I hit Delete, I opened up my Gmail again to stare into the abyss of my empty inbox. It was empty except for one spam email. Some political email from the White House. It was from Whitehouse.gov so I knew it was spam. Delete.

About two hours later, I saw I had five missed calls from my former publicist. That was weird. Five missed calls? So I called her back.

Before I could even get a word in, she said, very loudly, "They know you deleted *the email*, Carlos! Did you not read the email?"

Huh? What email?

"Carlos? Are you hearing me? They know you deleted it!"

"*Who* knows? What email? What are you talking about?" I said.

"The White House, Carlos. THE WHITE HOUSE KNOWS YOU DE-LETED IT."

I scrambled to my laptop. I swung it open so fast that I may have injured it somehow. I opened up Safari and typed www.ghail.com. *Ugh! That isn't the right website.* Then I typed it in correctly. I clicked a few times until I got to my deleted messages. And then I saw it. I had only one deleted email in my Bookings inbox from the last seven days. The spam one, the one from Whitehouse.gov. I dragged the curser over the deleted message and clicked it. The subject line had me shook: "White House Invitation."

Well, of course I deleted it! What in the world? Then I clicked it open . . .

> *Dear Mr. Whittaker,*
>   *The White House would like to formally invite you to give a few remarks and sing one song in the East Room of the White House on March 22. Thank you, Carlos, for the honor of this consideration.*
>   *Signed,*
>   *The Faith and Family Neighborhood Partnership Office of President Barack Obama*

Those blank lines represent the utter silence that fell over my entire being as I read those words.

"Carlos? Carlos! Did you read the email?

"YES! WHAT IN THE ACTUAL WORLD?"

A week later I found myself walking into the White House at six o'clock on a Tuesday morning. The Secret Service all but took my guitar apart on my way inside. I stood on a stage in the East Room practicing my sixty-second "sermon" and one song.

This is what was going through my mind: *The President of the United States of America is going to listen to my mini-sermon. The President of the United States is going to listen to my mini-sermon. The President of the United States is going to listen to my mini-sermon.*

A few things were still a mystery to me at that point, such as:

1. How did I get chosen for this?
2. How did I get chosen for this?
3. How did I get chosen for this?

At around half past eight, I walked into the restroom located in the basement of the White House and looked at myself in the mirror. Locking eyes with my reflection, I said, "You can do this. You were made for this. You got this."

I proceeded to walk upstairs and give a mini-sermon about the hymn "Nothing but the Blood" and then led the president of the United States, the vice president, and about one hundred other leaders in the hymn. I finished by saying, "Policies may help steer our country, strategies from this city may help steer our country, but nothing will save our country besides the blood of Jesus. Let's sing that chorus one more time."

During the next thirty seconds, the halls of the White House echoed with the words, "Nothing but the blood of Jesus" over and over again. I kept making eye contact with the president as he sang along.

How was it that this son of a black immigrant from Colón, Panama, was leading the most powerful man in the world in worship while speaking words into his soul?

Not only did I sing and speak, but I actually sat at the president's table and had an amazing conversation with him. I got to have a private meeting with him in the Red Room as well.

Friends, just seven days prior, I had driven into the parking lot of a Home Depot and sat in tears at the thought of going in to get an application. Nobody was calling or emailing me to book me for an event. Nobody wanted me anymore. And you know what? God was simply refining me in that moment. The growth did not happen when I got the email from the White House. No. The growth happened IN THE WAITING.

Heather and I walked out of the White House hand in hand. She was so proud of me. My very first gig after canceling my career was at the White House!

I was on cloud nine. "Babe! What in the world? I did it! And I heard a couple of 'amens' from the crowd! Did you hear them? And then how amazing was it when I had everybody sing a capella? I mean, how amazing was I!"

I went on and on for about ninety seconds as we walked across the lawn of the White House and out the east gate. I went on and on about how amazing I was. And listen, what I'm about to tell you actually happened. Everything in this book really happened. But I know how far-fetched it sounds. I wouldn't believe it if I didn't have a picture. As I continued my self-gratifying lovefest, forgetting for a moment that God was the one who had orchestrated this, I had taken about two steps out of the gate and onto public property when I felt something hit my shoulder. I looked over and saw a massive white blob.

"Babe! What the . . . ?"

Heather was dying laughing. "A bird just took a crap on your shoulder, Carlos. If I were you, I would immediately stop taking credit for everything that just happened and give the glory back to God before it ends up being worse than bird crap."

Did God send a bird to poop on my shoulder in order to remind me to give Him the glory? I have no idea. But I do know that I immediately stopped bragging and started praising Him. God gets the glory for our abundance, not us.

I obeyed. I suffered. And then I basked in the goodness of God's abundance. Friends, if you haven't yet seen the fullness of abundance in your life, don't give up. Keep waiting. Wild is on its way.

When was the last time God made you wait for a promise to be fulfilled?

REFLECT AND PRACTICE

1. In what small area of your life are you currently waiting for God to come through?

2. What is the biggest dream inside your heart that you would *love* for God to bring to life?

19

Adjust Your ISO

The camera is an instrument that teaches people
how to see without a camera.

DOROTHEA LANGE

Our relationship with God is not a math equation. One could take the teachings of this book and assume the following: Slow Down + Ask God + Hear from God + Attack the Lies You Hear from the Devil + Attack Them Again with God's Word = Step into Abundance! Although I believe these are the necessary steps to find true abundance, God is God, and He does not always operate in accordance with our expectations. But I do believe that if you follow this process consistently, you will find yourself swimming in more miracles, signs, and wonders than you ever knew existed. It is going to take work. You are going to have to do this thing for a while in order to see life to the full. Sometimes you might look straight into the face of Jesus and not even realize who He is. Sometimes we get so stuck in trying our own methods of getting healed that we don't believe Jesus could ever heal us. It's like the man at the pool of Bethesda in the gospel of John.

After this there was a feast of the Jews, and Jesus went up to
Jerusalem.

Now there is in Jerusalem by the Sheep Gate a pool, in
Aramaic called Bethesda, which has five roofed colonnades. In
these lay a multitude of invalids—blind, lame, and paralyzed.
One man was there who had been an invalid for thirty-eight
years. When Jesus saw him lying there and knew that he had
already been there a long time, he said to him, "Do you want
to be healed?" (5:1–6, ESV)

First of all, thirty-eight years is a long time. Thirty-eight years of wishing he could be free. When Jesus showed up, you would assume that He
could have just healed this man. But that's not what Jesus did. No. Jesus
actually *asked* the man if he wanted to be healed! What in the world? Why
would Jesus have done this? Who wouldn't have wanted to find healing
after thirty-eight years of suffering! Who would not want to enter into
abundance and wild after living without it for so long? There was obviously
a purpose for Jesus's question. And I think the reason is this.

Maybe the man didn't actually want to get well after all? Maybe he
had grown so comfortable in his affliction that he wouldn't know what to
do if he were suddenly well? Maybe his identity was rooted in his affliction? I don't know what his reasoning was. But I do know that so many
times I have grown comfortable in my affliction. When I think about the
anxiety I suffered with for so long until John helped me find freedom, I
wonder if it had become such a part of my identity that maybe I didn't
want total freedom from it. I don't know. All I do know is that Jesus asked
this man to tell Him if he wanted freedom before simply giving it to him.

The story continues, "The sick man answered him, 'Sir, I have no one
to put me into the pool when the water is stirred up, and while I am going
another steps down before me'" (verse 7, ESV).

There you have it. When Jesus asked the man the question whether he wanted to be healed, THE MAN DID NOT IMMEDIATELY SAY YES! Lord have mercy. When I read that part of the story, I wish I were standing next to that man so I could answer for him. "Um . . . what he means, Jesus, is YES! YES, he wants to be made well!"

Alas, the man didn't have a friend next to him to help him out. All Jesus got was an excuse. I read this, and I think how many times I have made excuses for my half-abundant life instead of just stepping into the fullness God has for me. How many times has Jesus asked me if I want to be made well and I am so comfortable on my mat thinking it would take too much work to trust that God can heal me? This man gave Jesus an excuse! Oh friends. Jesus wants you to be well. He wants you to *want* to step into the fullness and abundance and wild He has for you. BUT WE HAVE TO WANT IT! We can't just settle and endure whatever afflictions life throws at us. We must want a life of abundance in order to actually receive it.

"Then Jesus said to him, 'Get up! Pick up your mat and walk.' At once the man was cured; he picked up his mat and walked" (verses 8–9). Jesus told the man to rise. He did not bend down, pick him up, and stand him to his feet. No, Jesus told the man that he must pick himself up.

If I were him, I MAY STILL HAVE HAD DOUBTS. I mean, if I had been lying there for thirty-eight years waiting to be healed and then was told to stand up and walk, I would have some fear and doubt. It's possible I could have been healed yet not been able to trust the healing enough to stand in it. How many times have we been given abundance and continued to sit in our half-abundant lives because we don't trust what we've been given?

The only way to truly know is to stand up, pick up our mats, and walk.

I know this is a scary proposition. We get so comfortable with our mediocre lives. We don't want to be let down. We don't want to stand up only to fall back down and realize we haven't truly been healed. We don't want to be disappointed. But I promise you—no, HE promises you—get up, pick up your mat, leave half abundance behind, and walk into total abundance.

If I could sit down with each one of you reading this book, I would look you in the eyes and tell you that you can experience all God has for you right now. Not in five years when you have paid the penance for whatever sin you think is keeping you from Wild. Not in two months when you're feeling better or you've overcome whatever ailment you have. No. Right now. Right now you have the opportunity to Enter Wild.

Photography Lessons

A few years ago, my family and I were camping in the High Sierra. We were on the shores of Huntington Lake at nearly seven thousand feet above sea level. The days were warm and the nights were chilly—my favorite kind of climate. We water-skied in the lake each day and then sat around the campfire at night. The first night there was a storm rolling in so you couldn't see the stars, which was a bummer because the stars looked incredible that far away from the city lights of Fresno, California. The next day the storm had moved on, and the skies were clear. It was a glorious day, and we were rewarded with an incredible sunset.

Heather and I were sitting on the picnic table while the kids were doing who knows what in the woods behind us. Romance began to settle in the air, and I was certain I was going to get at least a thirty-second smooch out of this sunset. Then when the sun went down and the stars exploded above us, I was honestly wishing we didn't have a five-person tent. I draped my arm around Heather's shoulder and dropped some line like, "Is your mother a thief? Is your father a thief? Well, if they aren't, tell me this, my love. Who stole the stars out of the sky and put them in your eyes?"

To which she rolled her eyes and said, "Can you go grab the camera?"

Buzz. Kill.

"Can you grab the camera and take a picture of these stars? They are amazing."

Now I've seen incredible night skies before, but nothing like that one.

There were comets dancing, satellites moving, and galaxies pulsating. It was WILD in every sense of the word. There had to be at least thirty-two thousand stars. That's my guess because apparently I'm an astronomer now. In order to avoid ruining the closeness of our side hug, I simply grabbed my phone to take a picture.

"Babe. You can't take a picture of the stars with your phone. I think you need my camera." Heather had one of those fancy cameras with the buttons and dials and stuff. I took a picture of the stars with my phone anyway and got *zero* stars in the picture. She was right. So I got up, walked to the tent, and grabbed her camera. The romantic vibe of the evening was officially gone, but at least we could still get a halfway decent picture of the stars.

Now, I'm no photographer. I had no idea how to use all the buttons and dials on that camera. So when you don't know how to use all the buttons and dials on a camera, what mode do you use?

Auto mode. Of course. And why do we camera rookies put the camera in auto mode? Well, because we don't know how to use it and we know auto will at least take a picture for us.

So I set the camera on auto, aimed that puppy at the sky, and hit the shutter button. Look there! I see stars! Heather was right. Way better than my phone. So I walked over and showed her the picture.

"Babe. There are thirty stars in that photo. Look up. There are thirty million stars in the sky. I know that camera can capture the stars. We paid [insert too much money] dollars for that camera, right? Can you please, pretty please find out how to capture the stars tonight? *Pleeease?*"

And the next thing you know, I'm sitting on the picnic table with my phone out searching for YouTube videos on how to photograph stars. After watching a few horrible how-to videos, I decide to call a professional photographer friend in Nashville.

"Hey, man. Listen. I'm sitting here in the High Sierra trying to take a picture of the stars. I'm using Heather's Canon, but whenever I take a picture, I get about thirty-seven stars instead of the thirty-seven million stars that are actually above my head. What am I doing wrong?"

"Carlos," he said. "Is the camera in auto mode?"

"Um, yes. Why?"

"Because you can't take a picture of the abundance of stars in the sky in auto mode. It has to be in manual mode."

"Oh yeah, right. But I don't know how to do that. I don't know how to use it in manual mode."

"I know you don't. But I'm going to tell you how. It's the only way you will be able to pull this off. And listen. It's going to take some practice. But I promise you will get it."

"Okay," I said. I was totally not excited about having to take a photography class when I was trying to put the moves on my wife.

"First, you have to put the camera in manual mode. It's the *M* on the dial."

I was thinking, *I may be dumb, but I'm not* that *dumb.*

"Then you have to find the ISO setting, take it off auto as well, and crank that ISO up to 12,000. Then you have to find the aperture. It's actually called the *f*-stop too, but your camera will probably say 'aperture.' You have to lower it from wherever it is to about 1.2 if it goes that low. That is going to open up the shutter to the widest position so that the most light gets in, just as your pupils get larger in the dark. After you lower the *f*-stop you are going to have to find the shutter speed and lower that as well. You have to increase the amount of time that the shutter is open from a fraction of a second to like thirty seconds. That way the shutter stays open long enough for all the light to come in. Now if you do that you aren't going to be able to hold the camera, because when the shutter is open that long you will have to put it on a tripod or else it will be blurry. Got it?"

"Um. No. But I'll try."

"You got this, Los." He hung up, leaving me alone in manual mode.

ISO? Where is this ISO thing he is talking about? It took me five minutes to find the ISO. Then it took me five more minutes to figure out how to adjust it. And I think I accidentally adjusted two other things while adjusting that thing. And the *f*-stop? Or was it aperture? It took about five more minutes to find that, and it was at 8.2. Did he say to make it higher or lower? Ugh. Then the shutter speed. Took me another ten minutes to find that. I soon found that an hour had elapsed trying to TAKE A PICTURE of the stars. And every picture I took was *worse* than the one I took in auto mode. I kept taking pictures, and they kept coming out completely white.

Then I would readjust all the things, and not only could you not see the stars, but you couldn't even see the massive campfire in front of us anymore. The pictures were BLACK. I tried and failed, tried and I failed. And I tried and I failed again. Until . . . finally I took a photo with all the correct settings that my friend had now texted me because I couldn't remember. When I pulled the camera away from my eye and looked at the LCD display . . .

My jaw dropped. I couldn't believe what I saw. The photo was as close to Van Gogh's *Starry Night* as I'd ever seen. It was beautiful. Every single star in the sky was in that photo. The trees were lit up by the starlight, and there were even two meteor streaks across the sky. I was dumbfounded. I sprinted over to Heather and said, "BABE, LOOK AT WHAT I DID!"

And she smiled.

Guys. I was ready to quit my job as an author and become a *National Geographic* photographer. I had captured the abundance of stars that God had painted across the sky. Only I wasn't able to do it with the camera in auto mode. It had to be in manual mode.

YOU CAN'T LIVE YOUR LIFE IN AUTO MODE AND EXPECT TO ENTER WILD. You can't live your life in auto mode and expect to step into abundance. We walk around showing people the thirty-seven stars in our lives, so proud of them, while God is reminding us, *You don't just have thirty-seven stars! I have given you thirty-seven million stars! You just have to turn off auto mode!*

Friends, I know it's not easy. It is actually going to take work. But please, understand that what you have experienced this far in life is only a fraction of the WILD God has for you. We have become so accustomed to seeing only a glimpse of God's glory that we just accept it. Again, the purpose of becoming a Christian is not to simply wait for heaven. We get to experience heaven on this side of eternity. We don't have to wait to experience WILD.

Is it going to take practice? Yes. Will we sometimes pray and not hear anything? Yes. Will we ask and not receive? Yes. But keep adjusting. Keep asking. Keep changing the settings. Keep practicing. Because just as I experienced with that camera . . .

After failing to capture Wild many times, you will try one more time, and your jaw will drop when you see what has been waiting for you all along.

The Wildness of our great God.

REFLECT AND PRACTICE

1. Hearing? Trusting? Waiting? Which of these three would you say you need to spend the most time developing?

2. What do you feel is going to be the most complicated part of this newfound way of living?

20

The End

This is what GOD says,
    the God who builds a road right through the ocean,
    who carves a path through pounding waves. . . .
"Forget about what's happened;
    don't keep going over old history.
Be alert, be present. I'm about to do something brand-new.
    It's bursting out! Don't you see it?
There it is! I'm making a road through the desert,
    rivers in the badlands."

ISAIAH 43:16, 18–19, MSG

Let me reiterate something. Living the abundant, full, wild life God has for us does not mean that glory is going to fall 24/7. Remember, we are living in a broken world with trauma and trials. And oftentimes, we have to walk through the wilderness in order to truly Enter Wild. But we are able to receive God's favor and abundance even in the midst of those seasons.

I'm writing this final chapter from my hotel in Nairobi, Kenya. This chapter wasn't going to be in the book until yesterday. Why yesterday? Because yesterday God showed me what it means to Enter Wild in the most dramatic of ways.

I took my first trip to Africa ten years ago. Little did I know, I was about to enter the wilderness. Little did I know that my marriage was about to fall apart. Little did I know that I was about to lose everything. Little did I know that I was about to enter one of the hardest seasons of suffering in my life—with anxiety and depression. But when we got to Uganda ten years ago, life was good. Heather and I stepped off that plane in awe of this land and her people. We didn't know it at the time, but my seven-year-old, five-year-old, and three-year-old were about to have their lives shaken. And my nine-year-old marriage was about to end.

Yet sitting here now, in Africa once again, this time with my seventeen-year-old, fifteen-year-old, thirteen-year-old, and my wife of nineteen years, the following verse has never meant more:

> I am about to do something new.
>> See, I have already begun! Do you not see it?
> I will make a pathway through the wilderness.
>> I will create rivers in the dry wasteland.
> The wild animals in the field will thank me,
>> the jackals and owls, too,
>> for giving them water in the desert.
> Yes, I will make rivers in the dry wasteland
>> so my chosen people can be refreshed. (Isaiah 43:19–20, NLT)

Friends. WILD won't just be found in green pastures or when life is good. It's available in your desert too. It's been a hard decade for my family and me. We have faced pain, sorrow, disappointment, and lots of sadness. But oh, friends, we are promised deliverance. We are promised abundance. And even in your desert, WILD is right there waiting for you.

Remember, God is committed to our maturity, and nobody ever matures in the easy parts of life. Maturity comes in the desert. And we can do only so much in our own strength to set ourselves up for WILD. It wouldn't be WILD if we could pull it off alone, right? We need the mysterious, passionate, wild power of God.

Soul Safari

My entire family was in Africa for three weeks working with a few nonprofits. One of the final things we had planned was a safari in the Masai Mara National Reserve. The thing about safaris is that you have to save a lot of money to do one. You also have to get over the fear of being eaten by big hungry animals. You have to buy tickets, leave the comforts of your own home, and unless you live in a country where they run safaris, you have to leave your country. You have to make the effort to get up and go. And once you get there, you have to position yourself to experience the safari to the full. But that's all you have the power to do. The rest is up to God. Let me tell you what I mean.

When we initially talked to the kids about the trip, Seanna, our middle child, wasn't too thrilled. Not for any selfish reasons, but because she is simply a homebody. She loves to be home in her own world. She likes routine, but the rest of our family doesn't really live like that. She is also not much of a risk taker. She loves to know she will succeed at things, and she does what she is good at. She is the opposite of me in most ways. (However, she is a killer comedian, for which I take all the credit.) The poor girl has to constantly readjust her natural inclinations in order to handle the chaos of the rest of us. So when we told her that we were about to disrupt her world for an entire month, she took a deep breath, and then she exhaled slowly and agreed.

As if that wasn't enough, we then told Seanna, who sleeps in the van when we go camping instead of a tent because she is scared a bear will eat her, that we were going to go on a safari. And we would be sleeping in tents with armed guards. Game over. She was having none of that. Her fifteen-year-old mind raced with all the possible dangers of this safari. But she agreed to go. (She kinda had to.)

When we landed in the Masai Mara, our safari driver, Timothy, greeted us. "Greetings, my friends! Please come. Please come. I have tea and cookies waiting for you by our vehicle."

We followed Timothy to our vehicle, the Land Rover in which we were about to spend the next three days riding around this wilderness. There was only one problem. It had been built with no sides or windows. The seats were completely exposed. It was built like that so tourists could have 360-degree views of the wildlife.

We saw another safari vehicle driving down the road, and it was a fully enclosed van that had a pop-up roof. The roof was up and people were standing up in their seats looking through binoculars. I looked at Seanna and then at the van. I knew that's what she wanted to be sitting in, rather than in our mobile lion buffet.

We got in and started down the road. We stayed on the road and saw a family of elephants. We saw three giraffes. And we saw a bunch of Pumbaas! I know they are called warthogs, but *The Lion King* has officially ruined me. As we were driving down the road, Seanna was all but sitting on my lap.

"What if an elephant charges us?" she whispered.

I just kissed her head and held her tight. She was just going to have to trust Timothy. We all were. As we continued down the road toward the Kichwa Tembo Tented Camp, our home for the next three days, we saw more wildlife than we thought we were going to see the entire safari! No lie. Sohaila and Heather both cried numerous times out of utter awe. We saw them all. Zebras. Giraffes. Elephants. Hippos. And we hadn't even begun our safari yet!

We got to the resort and made our way to the "tents." I put that in quotation marks because these were the bougiest tents we had ever seen. They weren't really tents; they were buildings with two tent walls. And they were gorgeous. Like honeymoon worthy. The only problem was that, again, these kids were getting in the way of my romantic expectations. But we were together, and we were about to go experience something amazing.

We met Timothy a few hours later for our evening drive.

"Who's excited?" he shouted.

Four of us raised our hands. Seanna maybe lifted a pinky. We got to the top of the first hill, and Timothy stopped the truck. He pulled out his binoculars to scan the horizon. I saw him stop scanning and adjust his focus.

"Two male lions are walking across that field! Wow! Let's go find them!" And he put the pedal to the metal. We were flying down the hill toward the lions. They were about fifty yards from the road. When we got parallel to them, he said, "We are about to watch a story unfold! You see on the other side of us, across the road? There is a herd of Cape buffalo. This is incredible!"

And we looked over our shoulder, and sure enough there were about fifty buffalo. Seanna was once again on my lap. I secretly loved it. It was like she was five again. Then Timothy did something I did not expect him to do. He turned the vehicle and LEFT THE ROAD. He started driving toward the lions.

"Dad? Daaad? DAD! What is he doing?" Seanna whispered loudly into my ear.

"Just trust him, baby. He knows what he is doing. He would never put us in danger," I said, half trying to convince myself of it too. I immediately thought about the safari van that we had seen earlier that day. I would rather have been sitting inside an enclosed van at that moment, just in case the lions decided they wanted a human snack instead of buffalo.

Timothy proceeded to drive our Land Rover within ten feet of those two male lions. WITHIN TEN FEET! They had the same look in their eyes and the same stance as our cat at home right before he pounces on a bug. Only these were definitely not house cats. They weigh about 4,255 times more than our cat, Henry.

"Watch!" Timothy whispered with pure delight. "Watch closely!" He told us what was about to happen. "They will attack the herd in a few moments! Don't look away! This is incredible!" I could tell by the tone of Timothy's voice that even he was enthralled. This clearly wasn't something he saw every day. He knew we were witnessing the wild in a way that not everybody gets to experience.

Suddenly, I could feel Seanna relax. As the cats crouched and began to sneak toward the buffalo herd, she was just as enthralled as I was. She grabbed her phone, sat completely up, and started filming. Then it happened. One of the lions took off, and the herd of buffalo followed suit. That lion ran as fast as it could after those buffalo and finally caught up with them! I'm telling you, we were basically *inside* a Nat Geo nature special.

The herd of buffalo ran as fast as they could, putting the babies in the middle. They went left, and then the lion stopped. It stood still about twenty feet from them, staring at one hundred buffalo. Then a mama buffalo left the herd and RAN RIGHT TOWARD THE LION. You will never guess what happened next. THE LION RAN AWAY. That mother basically said, "If you want my baby, you are gonna have to go through me." And she won.

The five of us in the mobile lion buffet literally started cheering! Seanna was smiling and laughing! We all agreed it was one of the top moments of our lives witnessing that.

"Wasn't that just incredible?" Timothy shouted. He was so excited to be able to put us in a position to experience it. We continued on our way until we saw a herd of elephants about two hundred yards off the road and slogged our way through the mud to get to them. We got within twenty yards to keep ourselves safe and watched a baby elephant nursing. Again, it was magical.

As we drove away, I was kinda bummed that we couldn't get closer. Timothy had made me feel so safe in the wild that I literally had lost all fear! LOL. As we drove away toward the sunset, I was so grateful. Just. So. Grateful.

After pulling back into the tent camp, Timothy asked us, "Did you have fun?"

And I kid you not, Seanna, the one who had the most reservations about this adventure, yelled back the loudest. She was all in! Once she experienced wild with Timothy's guidance, it was magical for her.

We continued having the most magical of experiences. I told Timothy all I wanted to see the whole trip was a running giraffe. And the last morning we found a family of giraffes with a two-day-old baby and THE BABY WAS RUNNING! We also stopped right in the middle of the road because a family of elephants was walking right down the middle of the road toward us. I know I asked God to get us close to a family of elephants, but maybe not like this. They walked within five feet of the truck. We were all holding our breath. And then the matriarch of the herd turned her head toward me, looked me straight in the eye, tilted her head down as if to bow, and then continued walking. It was as if she was saying, "Here you go. God says Hi."

If I didn't have video of it, I wouldn't believe it. It's on my Instastory highlights if you want to watch how it all went down. I was stunned.

We drove up to a pride of lions in the middle of a field and watched them for a few minutes before they ran off. Even Timothy told us that we might have hit the jackpot of all safaris. We. Saw. It. All.

Seanna was no longer scared. In fact, she was now experiencing wild in a way she didn't even know she wanted! At the beginning of the trip, she wanted to be inside one of those enclosed vans. But Timothy explained the difference for her so well.

"Seanna, the vans may be safer, and you can definitely see the wild. But you are not truly IN the wild. You can see only when you stand up.

And even then you cannot see everything, The vans are also not 4x4 vehicles. They have to stay on the road. But in my car, I can drive you right up to the animals, and you can experience them in person, not from far away. And the drivers of the vans? They drive from the big city to here. They do not live among the animals as I do. So yes, you would have been safer. But you would not have really been in the wild."

I was stunned. Timothy's words to Seanna were a gift to us all. Seanna got past any fear she had of entering wild only when she trusted her guide. And when she did, even though it was still scary at times, she was able to experience wild in a way she never would have if she had she stayed safe.

And another thing. All Timothy could do was get us into position. Timothy didn't have a button in the truck that released the lions, that steered the elephants toward us on that road. He didn't have a button that released the baby giraffe and had it sprint at the exact moment we turned the corner.

No. That was God. We position ourselves to Enter Wild, and then God Himself is the one who delivers it.

Friends, that's why this book is all about getting you into position to Enter Wild. Once you are in position . . . you will never want to get back in that safari van again.

You ready? I am. Enter Rest, Enter War, and then Enter Wild.

I'll see you there.

REFLECT AND PRACTICE

1. How can you purposefully head toward WILD today?

2. Who can you tell about the WILD prayers you are praying? It's important to be intentional in bringing people into our WILD dreams and prayers so that they can support us while we wait.

3. Pray this WILD prayer aloud . . .

PAUSE AND PRAY

Father, Jesus, Holy Spirit,

It's time. Would You blow my mind today? Will You explode any sort of box I have ever placed You in and let those limits run wild?

I specifically ask that You reveal Yourself in every situation throughout my day. I ask You to turn my worry into wonder and my anxiety into amazement. I ask that You reveal to me where You have been trying to explode my faith and why I have been hesitant to do so.

Lord, will You show me desires in my heart that I did not even know existed? Lord, will You revive desires of my past that I have let lie dormant?

Explode revival in every facet of my life. I ask for miracles. I ask for signs. I ask for wonders. Show me Your face, Lord. And may I in turn show it to my world.

Help me Enter Wild. Amen.

My Daily Prayer

Father, Christ, and Holy Spirit . . . I come to be restored in You, renewed in You, and brought back to receive Your love and Your life and all the grace and mercy I need this day. Father, I honor You as my King and give every aspect of my life totally and completely to You. I give You my spirit, soul, body, mind, heart, and will. I cover myself with Your blood—my spirit, soul, body, mind, heart, and will. In all that I pray, I stand in total agreement with Your Spirit. I ask Your Holy Spirit to restore me in You, to renew me in You, and to lead this time of prayer. In all that I pray, I include [name your immediate family members]. Acting as the head of my family, I bring them under Your authority and covering as I come under Your authority and covering. I cover them with Your blood—cover their spirits, souls, bodies, minds, hearts, and wills. I ask Your Spirit to restore them in You, renew them in You, apply to them all that I now pray in their behalf.

Dear God, Holy and victorious Trinity, You alone are worthy of all my worship, my heart's devotion, my praise, all my trust, and all the glory of my life. I love You. I worship You. I trust You. You alone are life, and You have become my life. I renounce all other gods and idols [list those things that you have put your trust in], and I give You the place in my heart and my life that You truly deserve. I confess here and now, God, that this is all about You and not about me. You are the hero of this story, and I belong to You. Forgive me for my every sin. Search me and know me and reveal to me where You are working in my life. In the name of Jesus Christ, I ask You to reveal to me any lies or vows and strongholds that contradict Your Word and will.

Grant me the grace of Your healing and deliverance and Your deep and true repentance.

Thank You for loving me and choosing me before You made the world. I give myself over to You to be one with You in everything, as Jesus is one with You. Thank You for proving Your love by sending Jesus. I receive Him and all His life. Thank You for including me in Christ, for forgiving my sins, for granting me His righteousness, and for making me complete in Him. Thank You for making me alive with Christ! I bring the life and work of the Lord Jesus Christ over my life today, over my home, my family, my household; over all my kingdom and domain.

Jesus, thank You for coming, for being human like me. I love You. I trust You. I worship You. I give myself over to You to be one with You in all things—spirit, soul, body, mind, heart, and will. I receive all the work and triumph of Your Cross, death, blood, and sacrifice, through which my every sin is atoned for. I am ransomed and delivered from the kingdom of darkness and transferred to Your kingdom. My sin nature is removed, my heart has been changed by the Holy Spirit, and every claim being made against me is canceled and disarmed this day. I now take my place in Your Cross and death, dying with You to sin, to my flesh, to this world. I take up the Cross and crucify my pride, arrogance, unbelief, lack of trust and faith [and anything else you are currently struggling with]. I put off the old [insert your name here]. Apply to me and my family all the work and triumph of Your blood and sacrifice. I receive it all with thanks and give it total claim to my spirit, soul, body, mind, heart, and will. I bring the blood and sacrifices of Jesus Christ over my life today, over my home, my family, my household, my vehicles, my finances, over all my kingdom and domain. I bring the Cross, death, blood, and sacrifice of Jesus Christ against Satan, against his kingdom.

Jesus, I also receive You as my life. I receive all the work and power of Your resurrection through which You have conquered sin, death, judgment, and the Enemy. Death has no power over You, nor does any foul thing. I have been raised with You to new life, dead to sin and alive to God. With my family, I take my place now in Your resurrection and in Your life. I receive Your hope, love, joy, goodness, wisdom, power, and strength. Apply to me and my family all the work and triumph in Your resurrection. I bring the resurrection of the Lord Jesus Christ over my life today—over my home, my family, my household, my finances, my vehicles, and over all my kingdom and domain. I bring the resurrection and the empty tomb of Jesus Christ against Satan, against his kingdom, against every foul and unclean spirit, and I bring it upon every human being and their spirit, their warfare, and their household. I bring the resurrection and the empty tomb of the Lord Jesus Christ to the borders of my kingdom and domain, and I stake it there in the name of Jesus Christ.

Jesus, I also receive You as my authority, rule, and dominion. My everlasting victory against Satan and his kingdom and my ability to bring Your kingdom at all times in every way. I receive all the work and triumph of Your ascension through which Satan has been judged and cast down and all authority in heaven and on earth has been given to You. I take my place now in Your authority and in Your throne, where I have been raised by You to the right hand of the Father and established in Your authority. I give myself to You. Apply to me and my family all the work and triumph in Your authority and in Your throne. I give it total claim to my spirit, soul, body, mind, heart, and will.

I now bring the authority of Jesus Christ over my life today, over my home, family, household, vehicles, and finances, and over all my kingdom and domain. I now bring the authority, rule, and dominion of the Lord Jesus Christ against Satan, against his kingdom, against every foul and unclean spirit—every ruler, power, authority, and spiritual force of wickedness, their every weapon, claim, and device [name any foul spirits attacking you]. I send all foul and unclean spirits to the foot of the Cross for Jesus to deal with, together with every backup and replacement, every weapon, claim, and device, by the authority of the Lord Jesus Christ and in His name. I command the judgment of the Lord Jesus Christ on any spirit that refuses to obey and send those spirits to judgment by the authority of the Lord Jesus Christ and in His name.

Holy Spirit, thank You for coming. I love You. I worship You. I trust You. You have clothed me with power on high and sealed me in Christ. You have become my union with the Father, my counselor, comforter, strength, and guide. I honor You as Lord and fully give every aspect of my life totally and completely to You. Fill me, fresh Holy Spirit. Restore my union with the Father and Son. I receive You with thanks and give You total claim to my life.

Heavenly Father, thank You for granting to us every spiritual blessing in Christ Jesus. I claim the riches in Christ over my life today and over my family. I bring the blood of Christ once more over each of us—our spirits, souls, bodies, minds, hearts, and wills. I put on the full armor of God. The belt of truth, the breastplate of righteousness, the shoes of the gospel, the helmet of salvation. I take up the shield of faith and the sword of the Spirit, and I choose to be strong in the Lord and in the strength of Your might. I declare my dependence on You, and I take my stand against the Enemy and all his lying ways. I choose to believe the truth, and I refuse to be discouraged.

You are the God of all hope, and I am confident that You will meet my every need. I ask Your Spirit to send people to pray for us. I now call forth the kingdom of God, throughout my home, my household, my kingdom and domain. In the authority of the Lord Jesus Christ, giving all glory and honor and thanks to Him, in Jesus's name. Amen.[22]

Notes

1. *Vine's Greek New Testament Dictionary,* s.v. "anakeimai," http://gospelhall.org/bible/bible.php?search=anakeimai&dict=vine&lang=greek.

2. *Strong's Greek Concordance,* s.v. "zóé," https://biblehub.com/greek/2222.htm.

3. Rhett Power, "A Day of Rest: 12 Scientific Reasons It Works," *Inc.,* April 22, 2019, www.inc.com/rhett-power/a-day-of-rest-12-scientific-reasons-it-works.html.

4. MG Siegler, "Eric Schmidt: Every 2 Days We Create as Much Information as We Did Up to 2003," TechCrunch, August 4, 2010, https://techcrunch.com/2010/08/04/schmidt-data.

5. Jason Karaian, "We Now Spend More Than Eight Hours a Day Consuming Media," Quartz, June 1, 2015, https://qz.com/416416/we-now-spend-more-than-eight-hours-a-day-consuming-media/.

6. *Strong's Concordance,* s.v. "yatsab," https://biblehub.com/hebrew/3320.htm.

7. Carlos Whittaker, *Kill the Spider: Getting Rid of What's Really Holding You Back* (Grand Rapids, MI: Zondervan, 2017), 120–21.

8. W. F. Adeney, "The Great Confession," BibleHub, https://biblehub.com/sermons/auth/adeney/the_great_confession.htm.

9. To read more about these Gospel stories, see Mark 4:35–41; Luke 4:31–37; Matthew 21:18–22; and John 11:1–41.

10. Bethel Music, Jonathan David Helser, and Melissa Helser, "Raise a Hallelujah," *Victory,* Bethel Music, 2019.

11. Elyssa Smith, UPPERROOM, "Surrounded (Fight My Battles)," *To the One,* The Fuel Music, 2019.

12. *Blue Letter Bible,* s.v. "anthistēmi," www.blueletterbible.org/lang /lexicon/lexicon.cfm?t=kjv&strongs=g436.

13. Material adapted from Whittaker, *Kill the Spider,* 193–94.

14. "6 Benefits of Beetroot Juice: Why You Should Drink It Every Day," NDTV Food, August 21, 2018, https://food.ndtv.com/health/6 -incredible-beetroot-juice-benefits-why-you-should-drink-it-every -day-1656806.

15. Chester and Betsy Kylstra, *Biblical Healing and Deliverance: A Guide to Experiencing Freedom from Sins of the Past, Destructive Beliefs, Emotional and Spiritual Pain, Curses and Oppression* (Ada, MI: Chosen Books, 2014), 33.

16. *Merriam-Webster,* s.v. "forgive," www.merriam-webster.com /dictionary/forgive.

17. *Merriam-Webster,* s.v. "pardon," www.merriam-webster.com /dictionary/pardon.

18. Jacqueline Howard, "Forgiveness and Your Health: What Science Says About the Benefits," CNN, June 5, 2019, www.cnn.com /2019/06/05/health/forgiveness-health-explainer/index.html.

19. Dr. Caroline Leaf, "Why You Should Embrace the Forgiveness Mindset," Thrive Global, August 2, 2018, https://thriveglobal.com /stories/why-you-should-embrace-the-forgiveness-mindset.

20. Chester and Betsy Kylstra, *Biblical Healing and Deliverance,* 33–34.

21. C. S. Lewis, *The Lion, the Witch and the Wardrobe* (New York: HarperCollins, 2000), 48.

22. This prayer was taken from *Walking with God* by John Eldredge. Copyright © 2008 by John Eldredge. Used by permission of Thomas Nelson, www.thomasnelson.com. The prayer was adapted from the version found on pages 221–25 of *Walking with God: How to Hear His Voice* (Nashville, TN: Thomas Nelson, 2016).